Carving Miniature Animals

with Debbie Barr

Text written with and photography by Jeffrey B. Snyder

Schiffer Publishing Ltd®

4880 Lower Valley Road, Atglen, PA 19310 USA

I would like to dedicate this book to Verna Leith, whose dream and purpose of the Sawmill Center for the Arts is to promote and preserve traditional handcraft skills. To encourage and provide for the study and practice of wood carving and other fine arts to all persons interested in acquiring such skills. A place where nature truly meets the Arts.

It is with my deepest gratitude that I dedicate this book to her.

Also, my sincerest thanks to all the past and present Sawmill Center Staff for their enthusiasm and support.

Library of Congress Catalog Card Number: 99-62298

Book Designed by Bonnie M. Hensley
Type set in Seagull Hv BT/ Swis721BT

ISBN: 0-7643-0936-6
Printed in China

Published by Schiffer Publishing Ltd.
4880 Lower Valley Road
Atglen, PA 19310
Phone: (610) 593-1777; Fax: (610) 593-2002
E-mail: Schifferbk@aol.com
Please visit our web site catalog at
www.schifferbooks.com

This book may be purchased from the publisher.
Include $3.95 for shipping. Please try your bookstore first.
We are interested in hearing from authors
with book ideas on related subjects.
You may write for a free printed catalog.

In Europe, Schiffer books are distributed by
Bushwood Books
6 Marksbury Avenue
Kew Gardens
Surrey TW9 4JF England
Phone: 44 (0)181 392-8585; Fax: 44 (0)181 392-9876
E-mail: Bushwd@aol.com

Contents

Acknowledgments

I am extremely grateful to several individuals who encouraged and supported me as a woodcarver through the years. These people have given me good advice and have listened to my ideas (both good and bad). They have also helped me with their positive attitude and with their urgings. Because of them, this book is a reality.

My sincerest thanks to:

Tom Wolfe for his advice, his support, and for challenging me to develop and explore my own individual style and creativity.

Harold Enlow for his encouragement and advice. Harold introduced me to the world of caricature carving.

Desiree Hajny for her enthusiasm and support.

To Professor Bob Butler, a master carver who was the first to inspire me as a wood carver, to advise and challenge me with positive criticism, to encourage me to develop my own creativity. Professor Butler continues today to share his great enthusiasm for wood carving.

To my husband Dick and the kids, Sean, Keli, Rob, and Jay for their continued support and encouragement ... and for putting up with the endless trails of wood chips!

To Dad, Mom, and my family for their support.

To my friend Barb, whose advice and support I couldn't do without.

For my carving buddy Jim Kilby and other carving friends for their support and for the fun times we have carving together.

Introduction

As far back as I can remember, I have spent time walking, sitting, or playing in the woods, meadows, or fields surrounding my home. I was fascinated by the animals that lived in those wild places. I spent hours watching them play, gather food, or just scamper around. Later, those early observations of wildlife came in very handy when creating engaging animal carvings.

Larger carvings often leave behind sizable wood scraps and tag ends. I have found that these scraps are ideal materials from which to carve miniature animals, all curled up, some sleeping and others wide awake. I have found that a variety of easily carved woods lend themselves to these small carvings, including basswood, butternut, and walnut.

Keep in mind, whether your animal carvings are on the small or large scale, that the animal's structure and the proportions of the head to the body must be correct if the carving is to look natural. Study and research the animals you wish to carve. Find pictures featuring the animal in a variety of poses. Books on animal structure and video tapes are also useful references. If you are able, try to see the real, live animals in your back yard, in the woods, or at the zoo. All this research, both in the books and in the field, will help to enrich your carving.

Tools

These are the tools I use to create the animal carvings found in this book:
a set of carving knives (I prefer a set hand made by Tom Wolfe), gouges (1/4 #7; 5 mm #9; 3/4 #7; 3/16 #5), V tools (1/4" and 1/8"), veiners (3/16"; #2; #1), Woodcraft carver's eye punches, a wood burner (mine is a Detailmaster) with 5 and 11A tips for animal fur, and reference books and drawings (including *Drawing the Animal* by Jack Hamm and *National Audubon Society Field Guide to North American Animals*).

To paint my animal carvings, I use:
oil paints mixed with turpentine (squirrel colors: white, black, gray, and Burnt Sienna; mouse colors: brown, white and pink) and Deft Spray or Watco Natural Oil.

I hope you enjoy carving these comical, fun little animals as much as I do!

Debbie Barr

Carving Projects

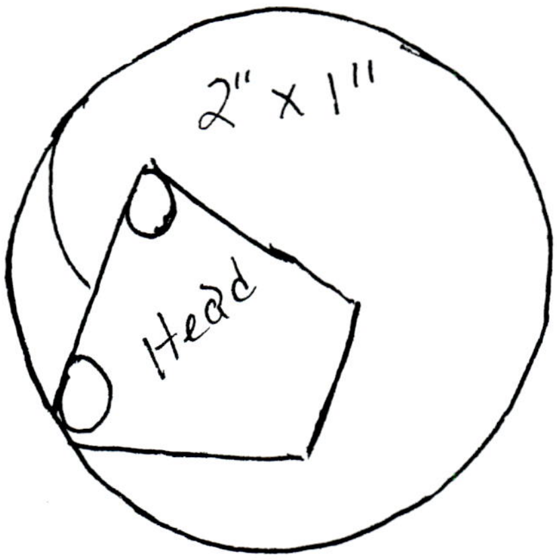

Here is the squirrel we will carve and paint.

Carving the Squirrel

Use a 2" diameter and 1" deep circular basswood blank (or hardwood blank, if you prefer) to begin carving the squirrel. I like these projects because very little wood is needed to complete them.

Draw in a line to indicate the curvature of the spine, showing how the animal is laying down. The pencil is located at the intersection between the spine and the back of the head.

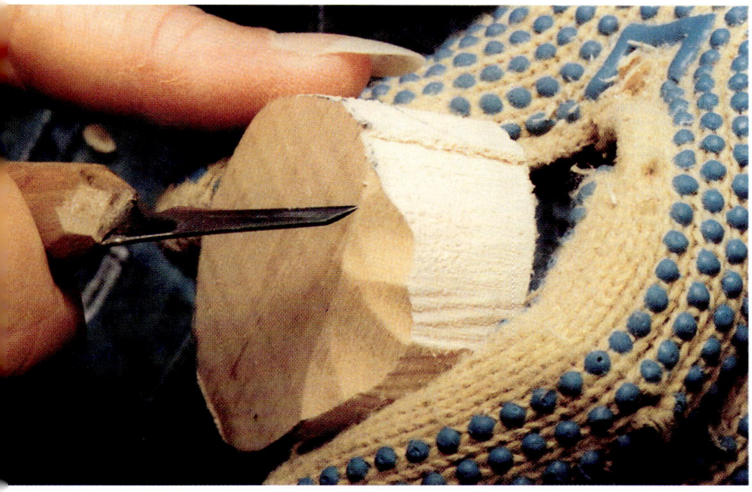

Begin rounding the top of the blank, forming a domed shape.

Place a stop cut around the outline of the head, using the carving knife.

Determine which way the head will be turned and then draw in a trapezoidal rectangle to show the positioning of the head. The small end is the nose, the large end is the back of the head.

Start removing the excess wood from around the head.

Continuing to remove excess wood from around the head, making the head stand up well above the body.

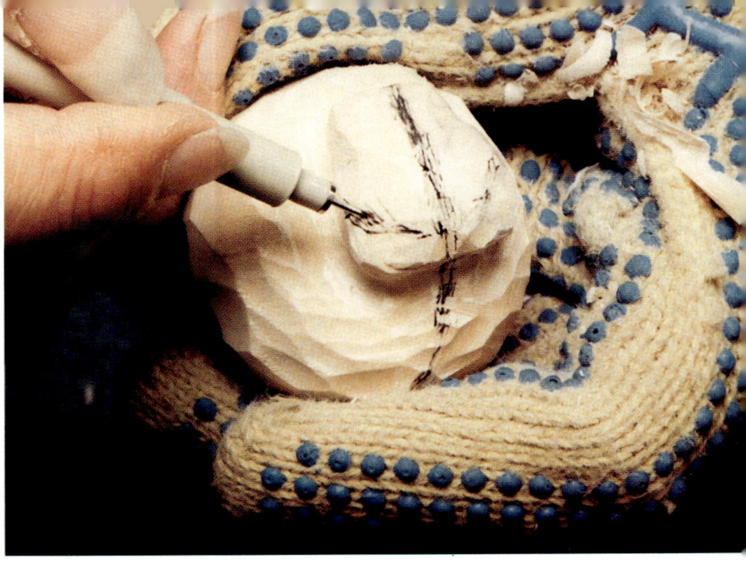

Draw in where the ears will go.

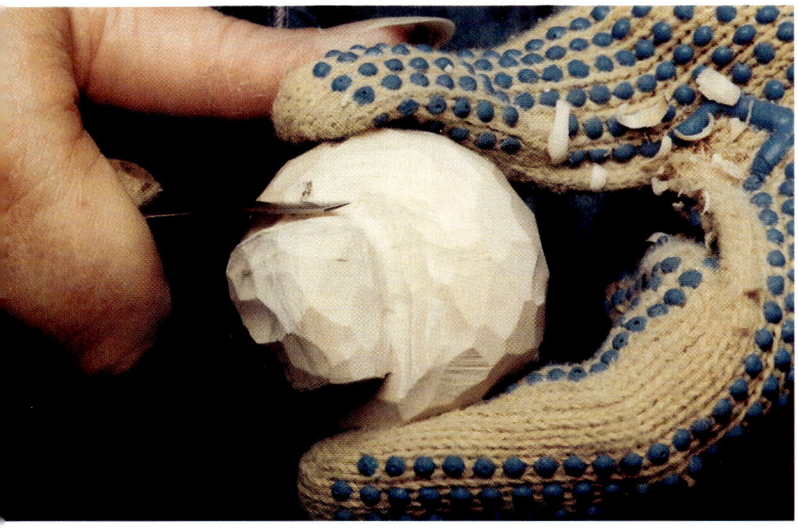

The excess wood is removed from around the head.

The nose is too wide. Round the corners of the muzzle.

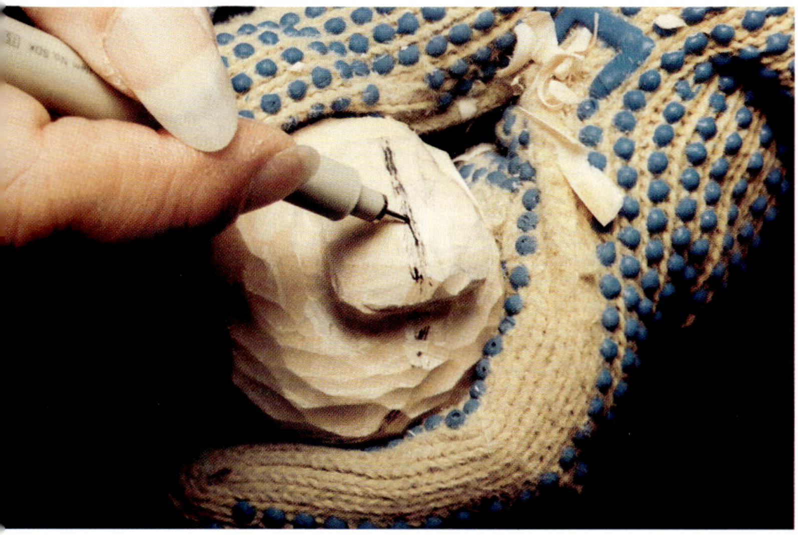

Draw in the centerline along the head and the body. Reestablish this guide line as you carve.

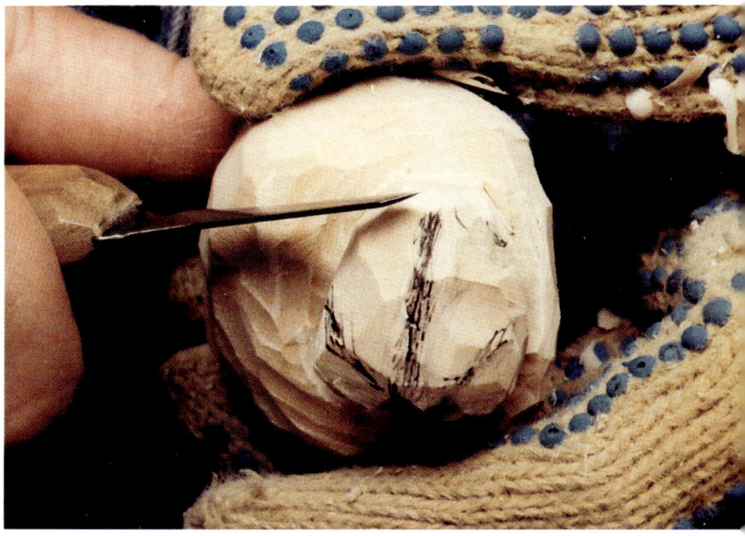

The muzzle is rounded.

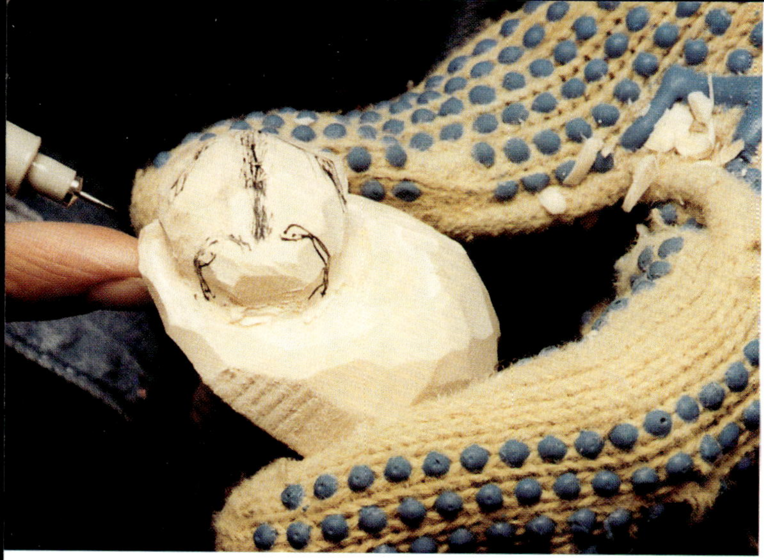

Draw in the lines for the mounds around the mouth.

Continue to round the head.

Use a 3/16" veiner, follow the pattern line for the curve of the nose and the mouth.

Use the carving knife to make a diagonal cut in front of the ears, which is the temple area.

Further round the muzzle.

Here is the ear mound.

The ears are raised high on the side of the squirrel's head. The insides of the ears are turned to the outside of the head.

Take the veiner and shape around the outside of the ear, giving it form and roundness.

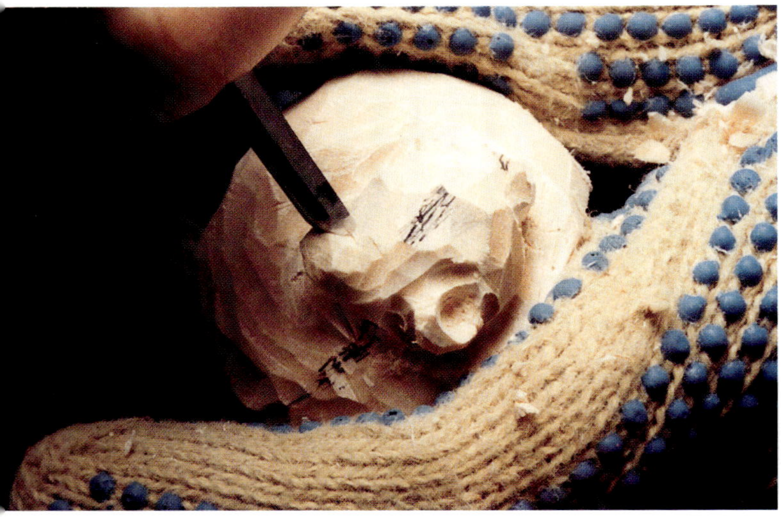

Use the 3/16" veiner to very carefully hollow out the insides of the ears.

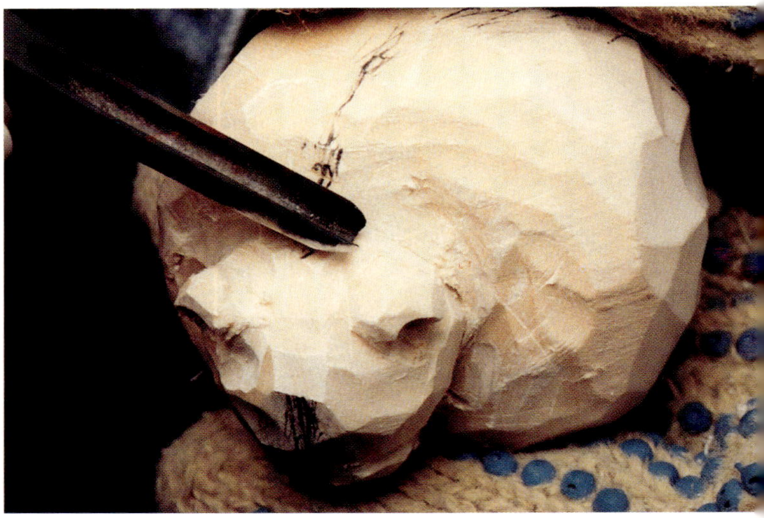

The ear is rounded.

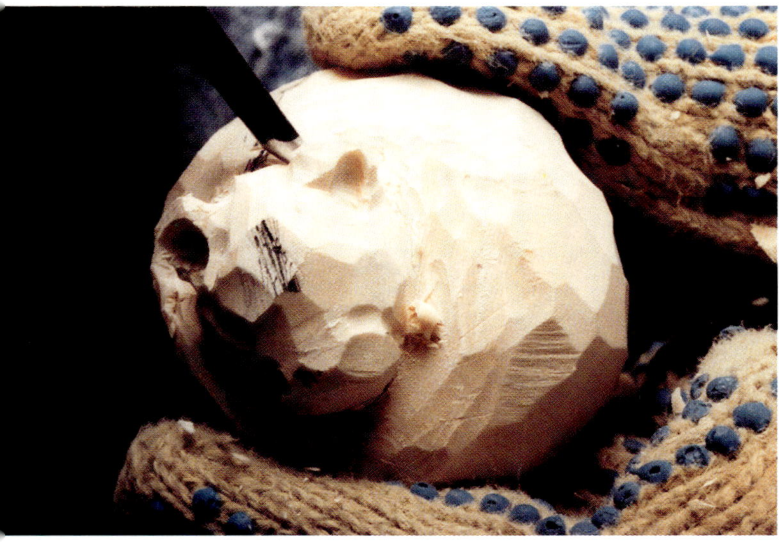

The hollowed out ears.

Use a #2 veiner or the 3/16" veiner and hollow out along this line for the area of the eye and the side of the head.

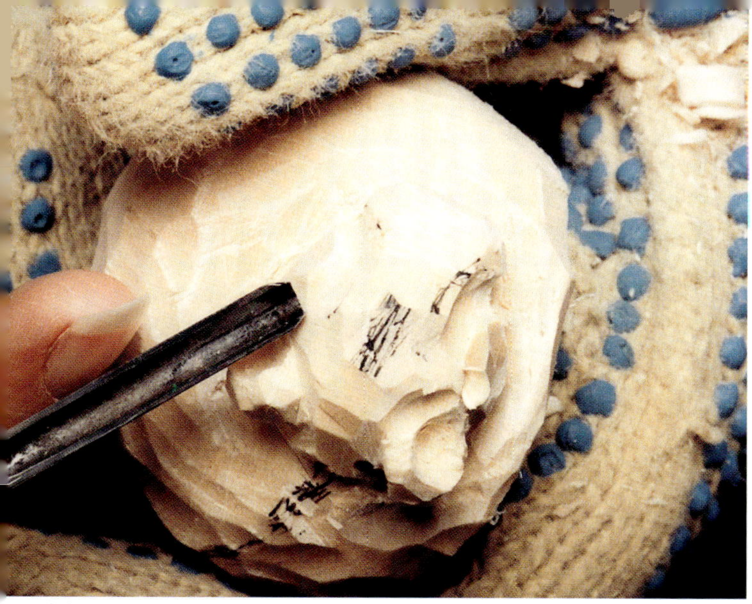

Like this. (The ears are at the bottom of the photograph and the tip of the nose is along the top of the image.)

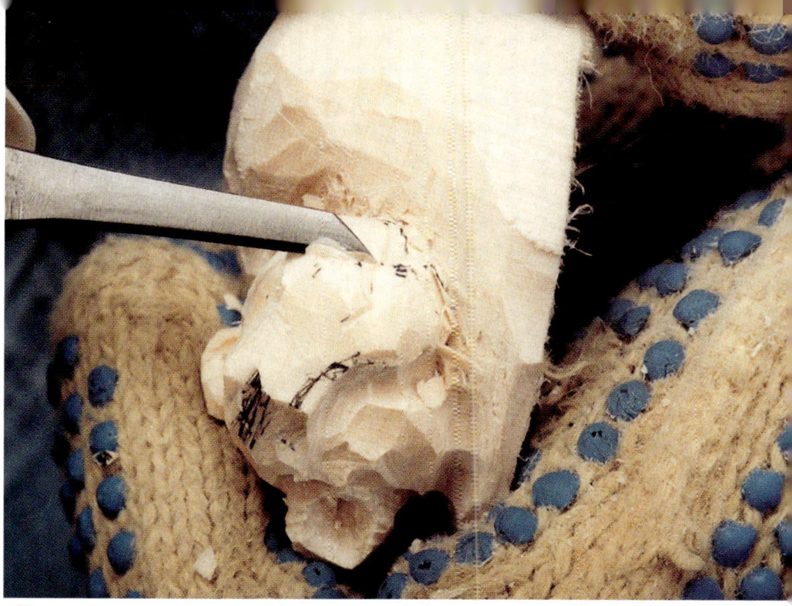

Removing excess wood from around the nose to make it stand up a bit.

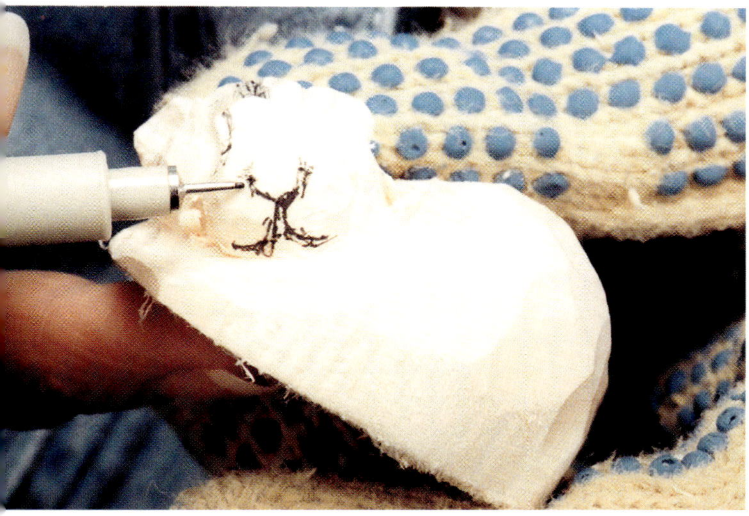

Draw in the lines around the nose and mouth.

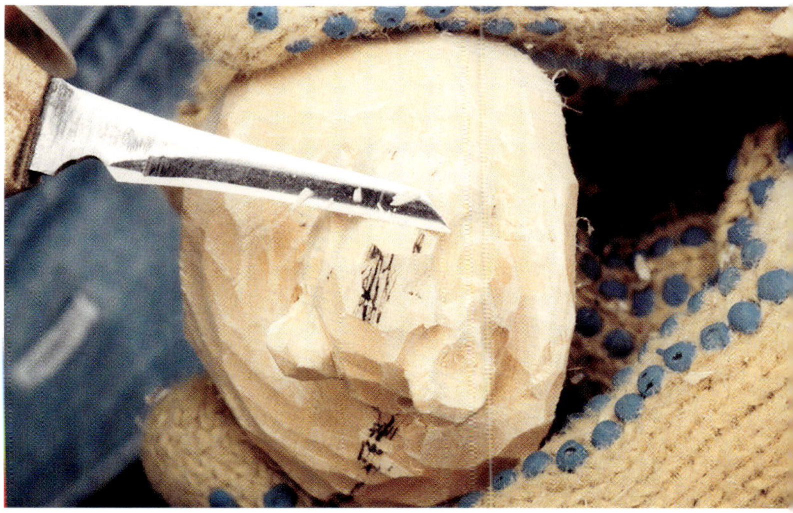

Hollowing out the bridge of the nose.

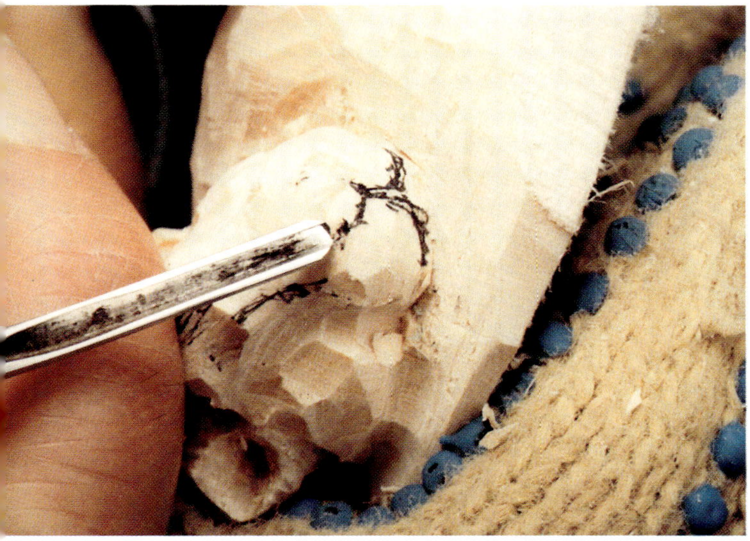

Use a V tool or a knife to cut along the lines drawn for the nose and mouth, forming these features.

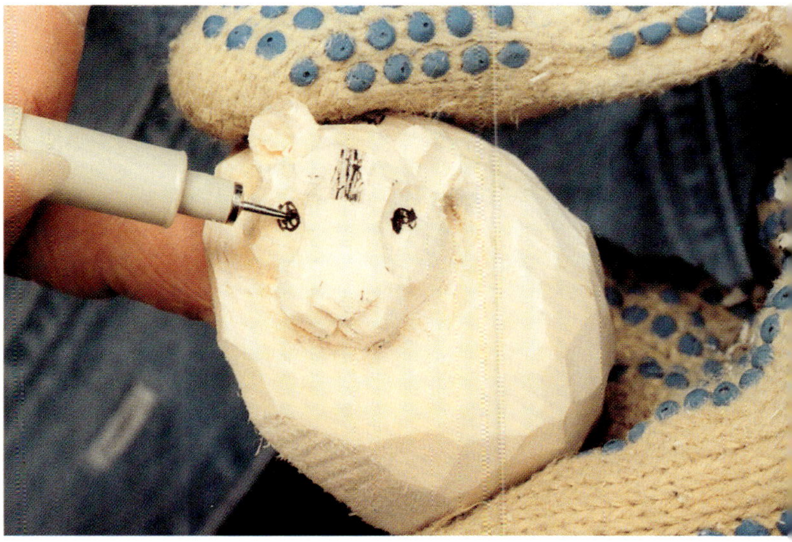

Mark in the eyes, they are located half way between the tip of the nose and the back of the head. Squirrels' eyes are located a little higher on the side of the head.

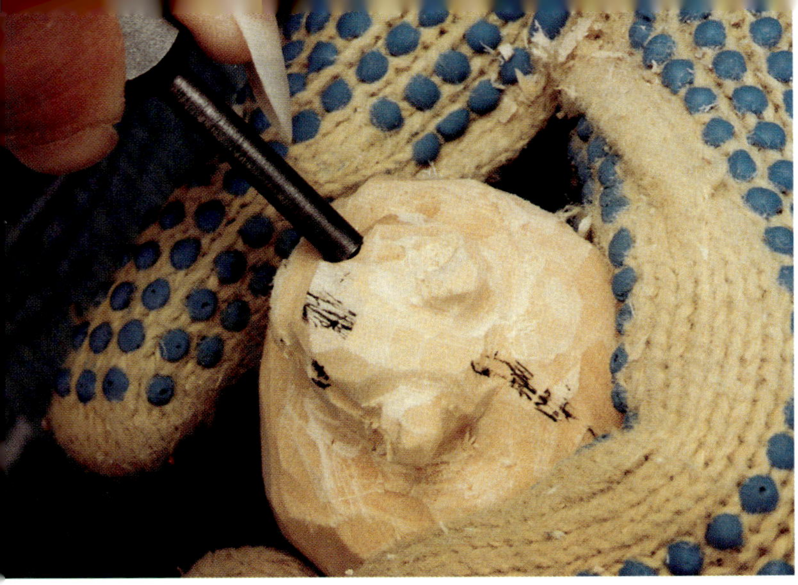

I'm using the Woodcraft 5/32" eye punch to create eyes on the squirrel. Make sure both eyes are positioned the same distance and height from each other, and both at the same angle. The eye is punched into place.

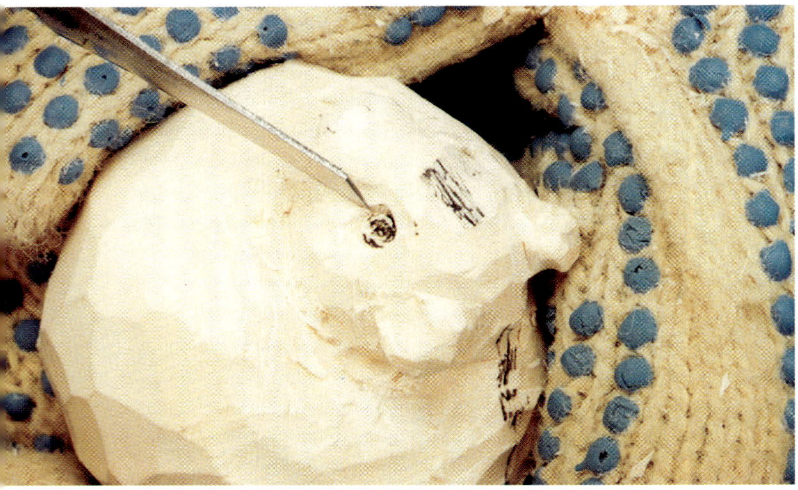

Carve a little triangular shape into the front corner of the eye for a tear duct.

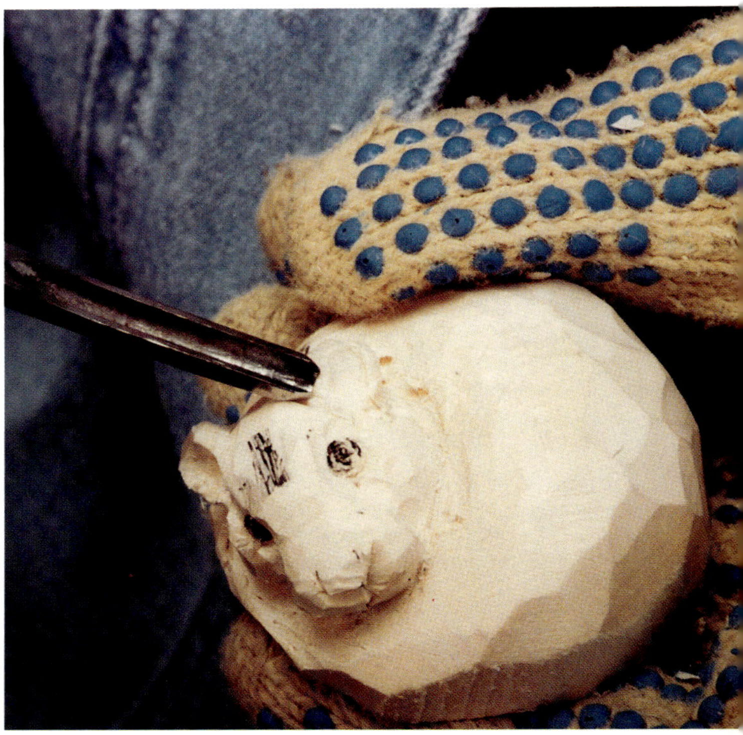

Using a veiner, go around the front of the ear along the temple to create a hollow.

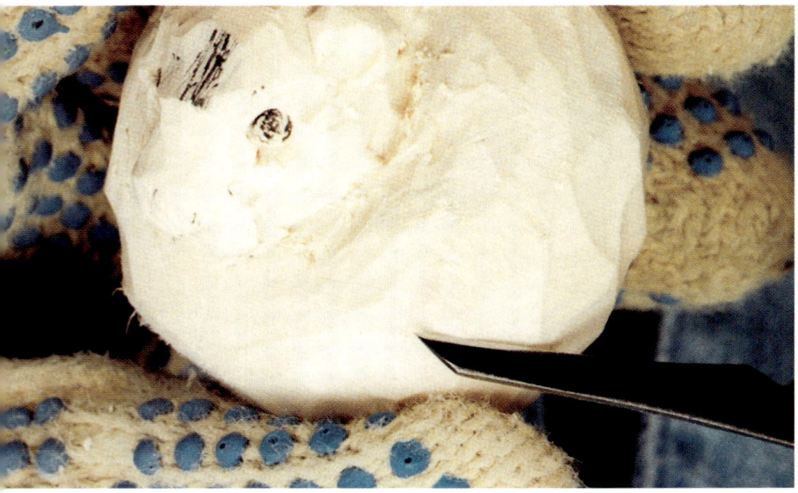

The triangle is in place. The wood from within the triangular cut has been removed, revealing the tear duct.

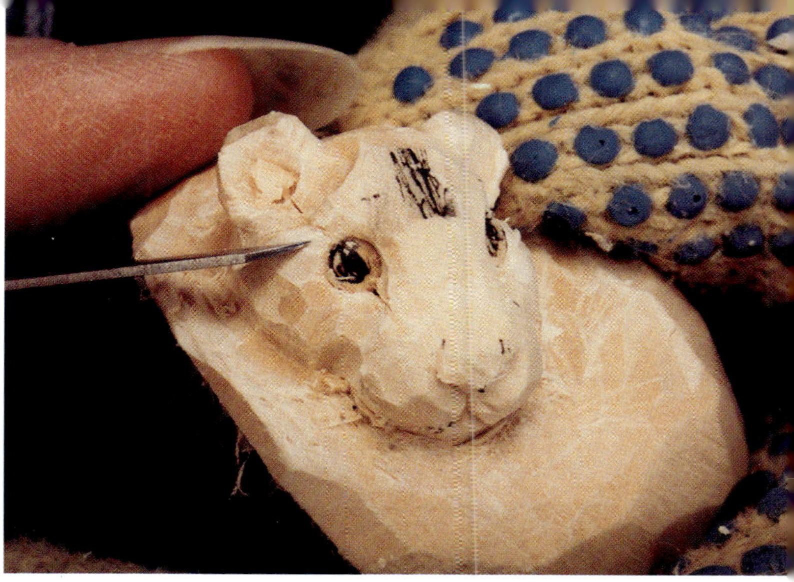

Cut a stop cut in the area behind the eye and undercut the line with a carving knife.

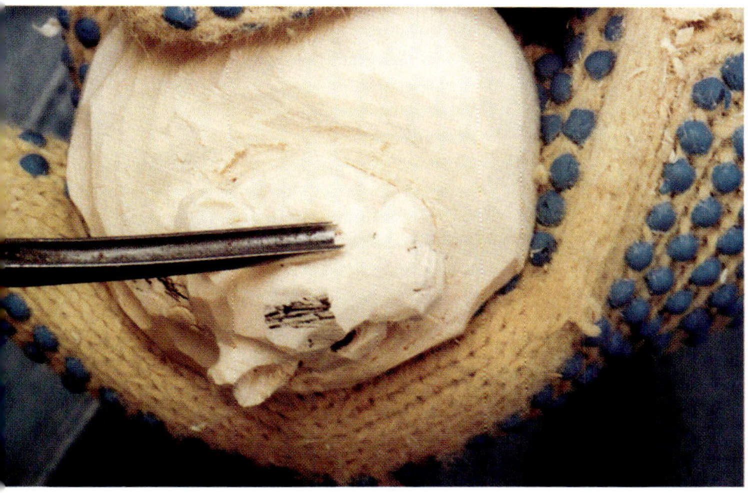

There is also a hollow in front of the eye, down along the nose. Use a veiner to create these hollows on either side of the head.

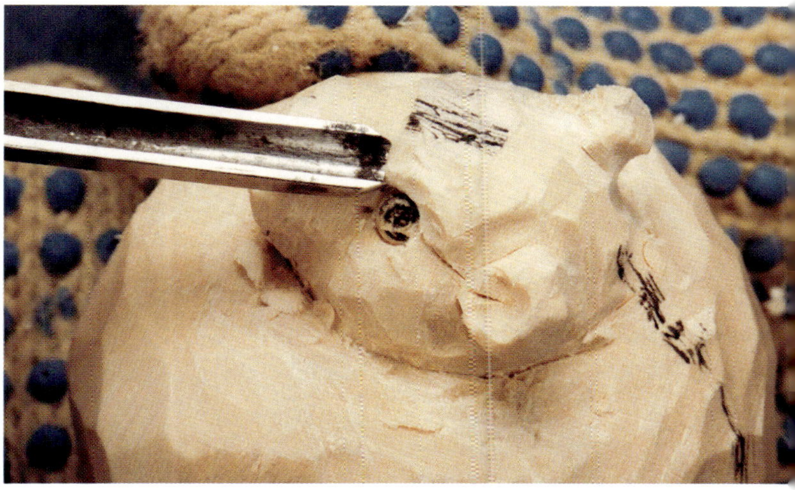

Use the veiner to cut a line both above the eye and below them to create the bone structure around the eye.

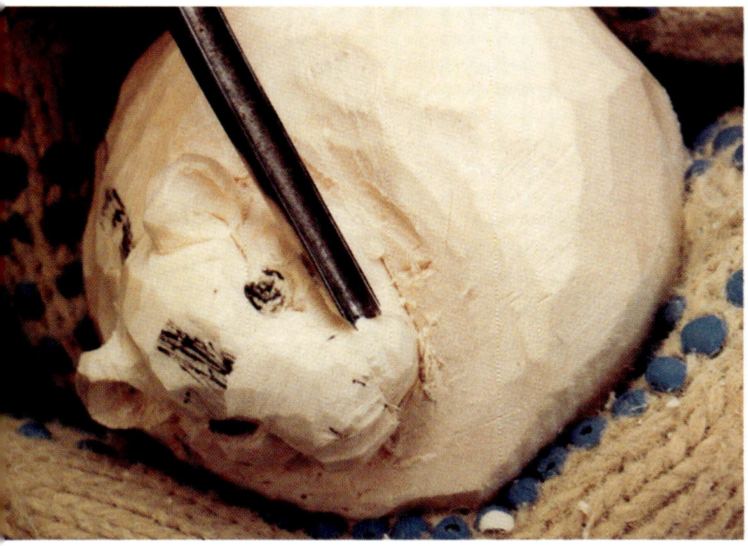

Also use the veiner to create hollows along the sides of the nose.

The bony structures (the orbits) around the eyes are in place.

The carving of the head is complete, ready for wood burning. Now let's move on to the body.

Draw in a guide line separating the right front shoulder from the body.

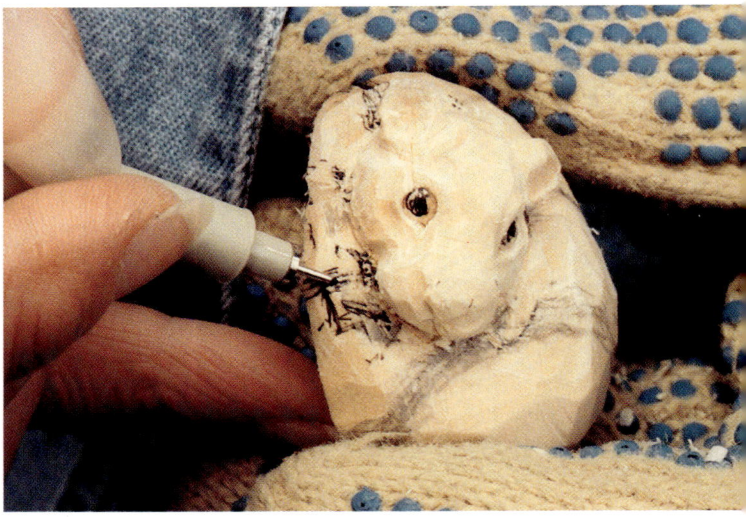

Draw in the location of the front left paw extending out from under the squirrel's head. The squirrel's front paws are crossed.

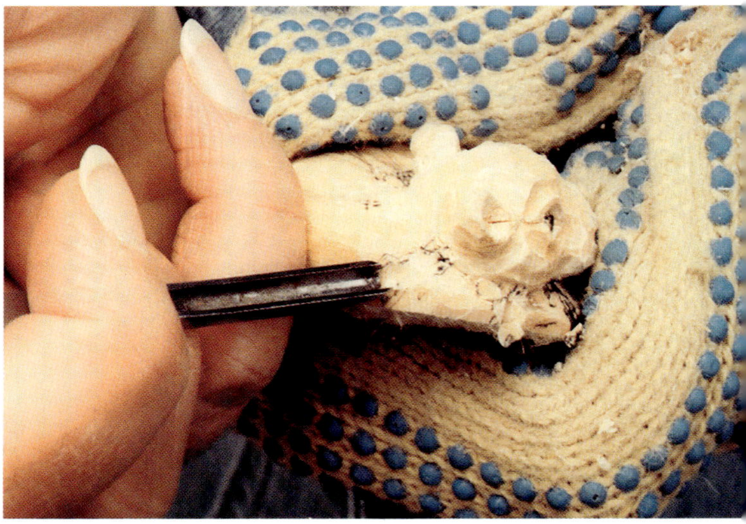

Use the veiner to cut in a shallow line for the shoulder.

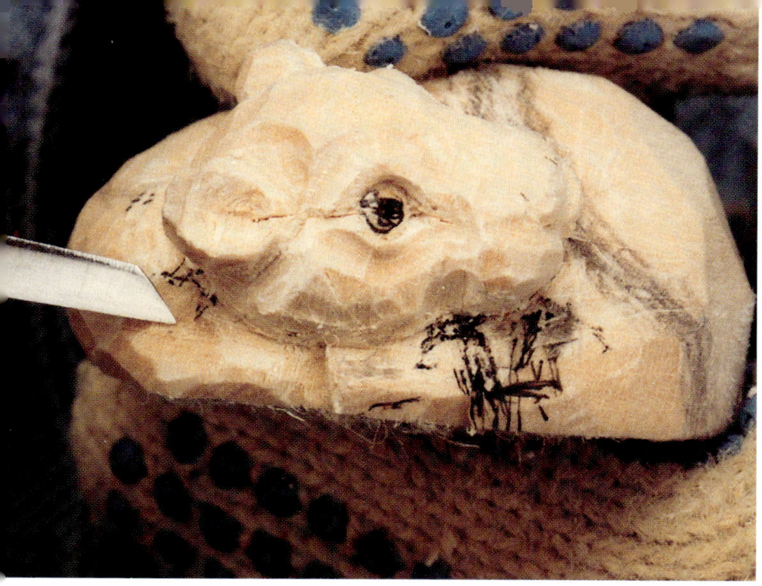

Use the knife to round the shoulder; get the angle of the elbow in place as well.

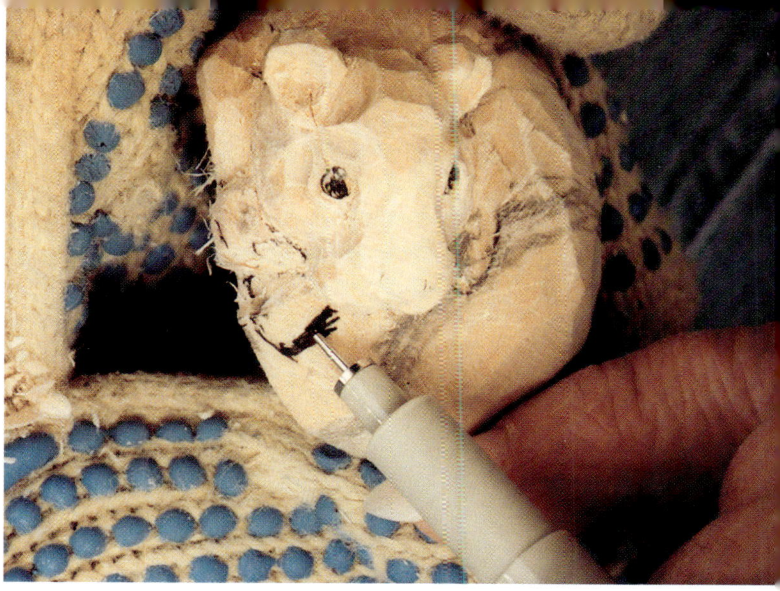

Draw in the right front paw, making sure it is in line with the carved shoulder.

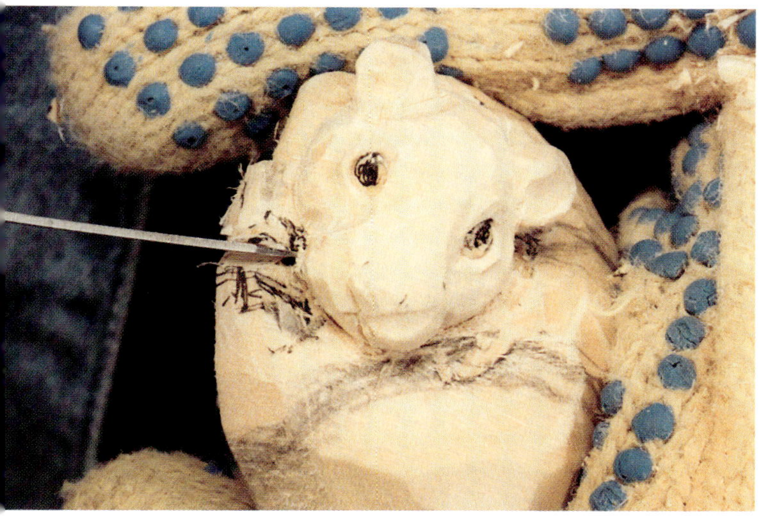

Begin to remove excess wood from around the left front paw.

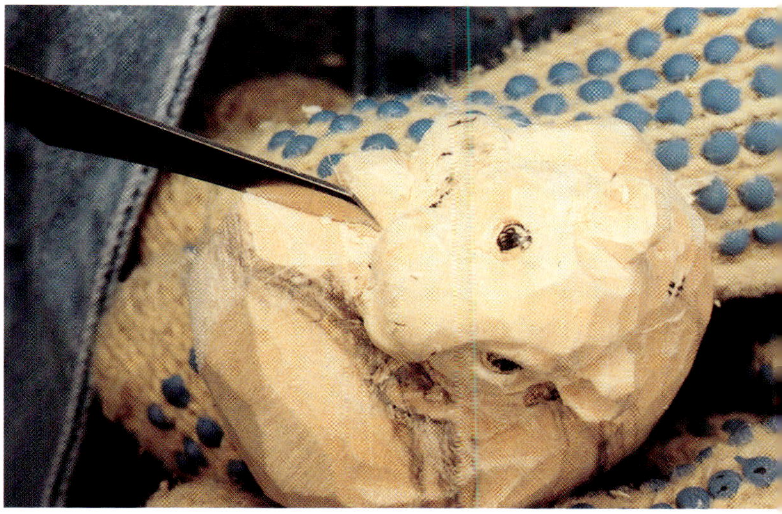

Carve in the right front paw with the knife, making sure the paw appears to be extending out from under the left front paw.

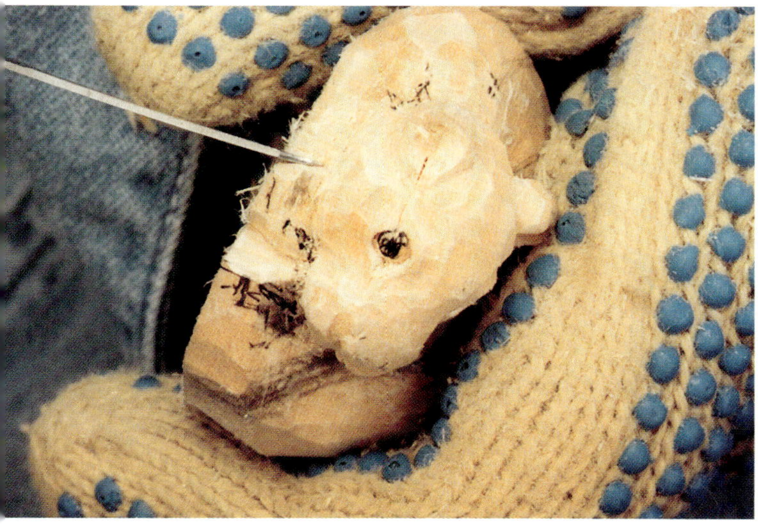

The paw is now carved into place.

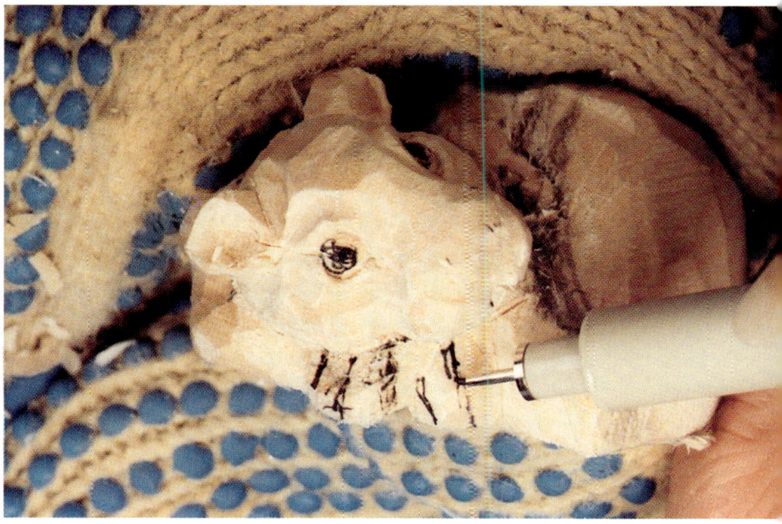

Draw in the lines indicating the separation between the toes on each paw.

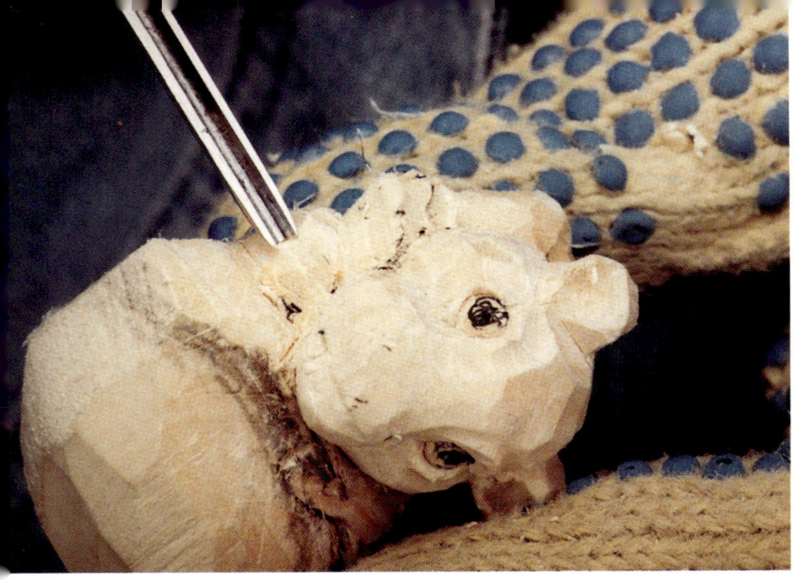

Use a #1 veiner and follow these lines to create the separations between the toes. Of course, you can use any tool that works for you. Carve in the claws. We will indicate the toenails later with the wood burner.

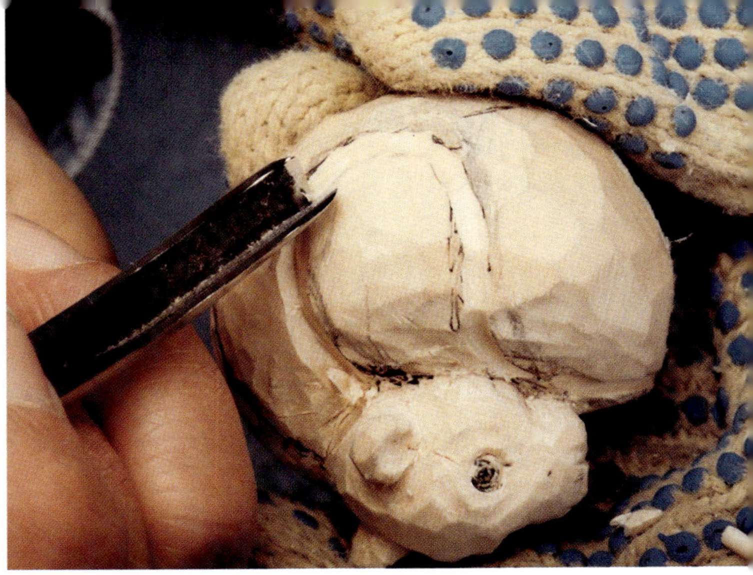

Use a 1/4" V tool to outline around the hip area and the tail, following your guidelines.

Reestablish the curve of the spine.

Use a 1/4" #7 gouge to remove the background wood, letting the hip stand up higher than the back.

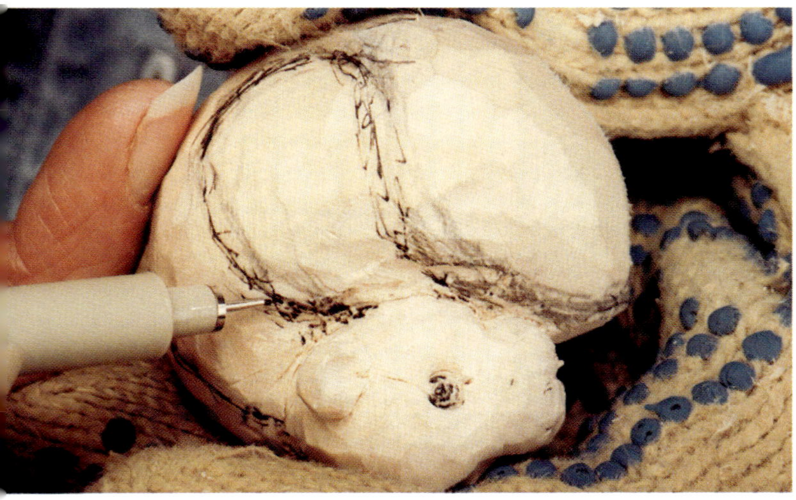

Draw in lines indicating both the line of the hip and the curve of the large, fluffy tail.

Repeat this process on the top of the hip to raise the tail above the hip, as seen here.

Remove the wood around the tail to establish the location of the stomach.

Using a V tool, follow the line of the foot, establishing a stop cut line.

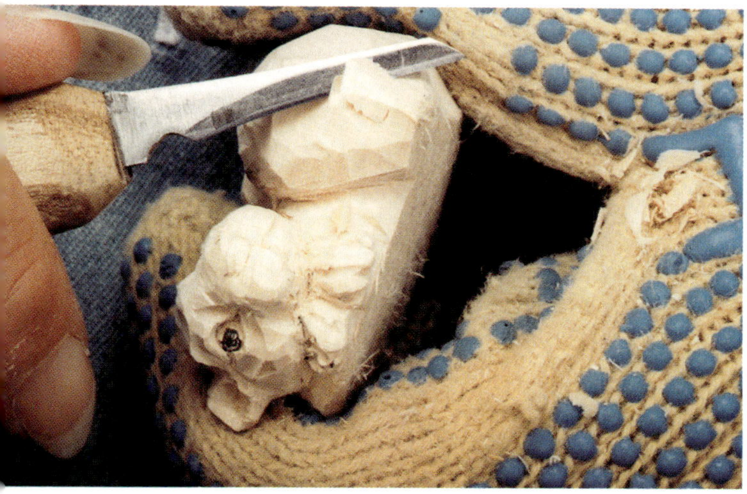

Shape the tail.

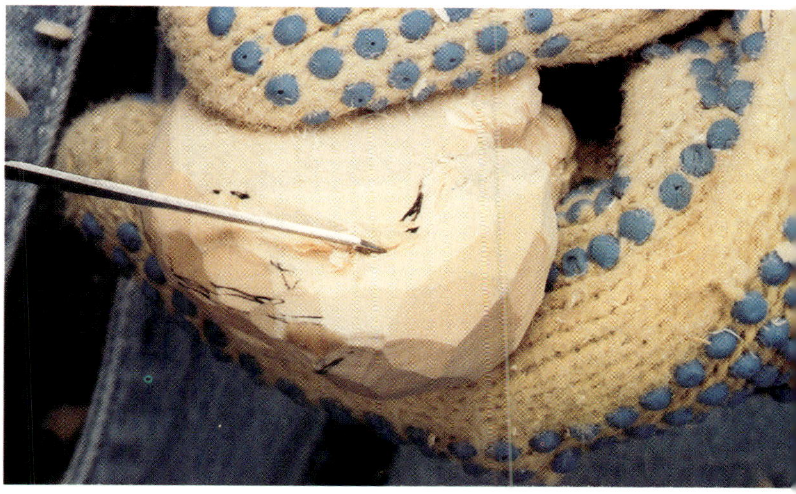

Use a knife to carve away excess wood around the left rear foot.

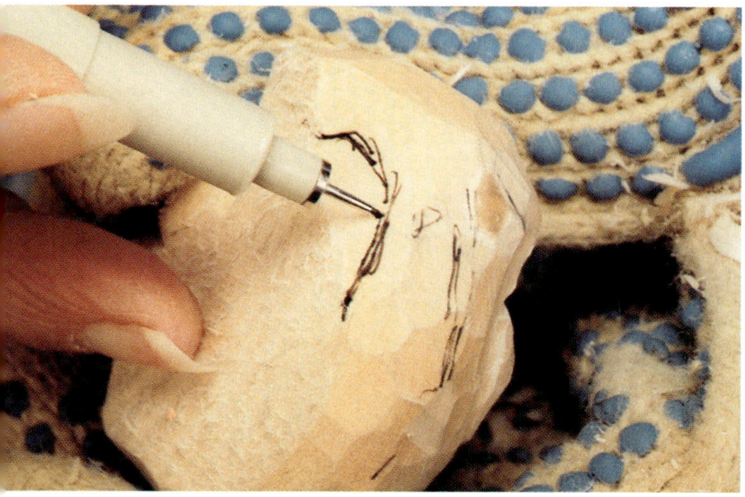

Establish the line of the left back foot sticking out beneath the tail.

Use a 1/4" #7 gouge to continue to remove excess wood from around the rear foot and to smooth the curve of the tail.

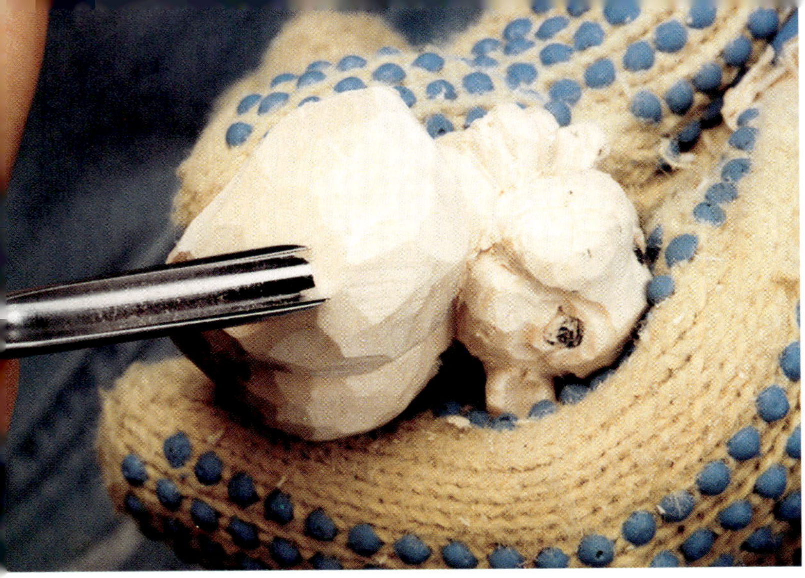

Use a 5 mm #9 gouge (or whatever tool works for you) to give the tail some depth by creating separate masses of fur.

The fur on the tail is in place.

Like so.

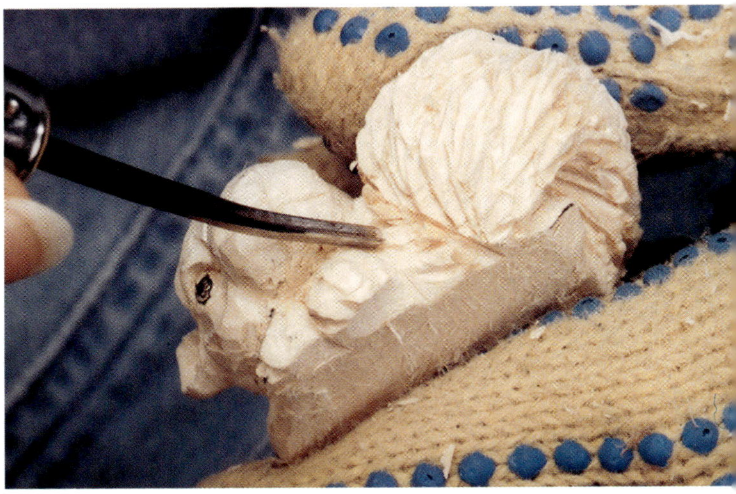

Fuzz up the belly a bit as well.

Take a small V tool or veiner to create fur tracks in the tail to further define the fur. Never make parallel lines, criss-cross them to follow a natural hair growth pattern. Study the fur on animals to make this look natural. The hair should not be all straight or it will look combed.

Carve in a little fur around the cheeks and the face.

We have carved as much as we need to at this point. We will add additional fur texture to the body of the squirrel with the wood burner using #5 and #11A tips. Any wood burner with variable temperature control will work well.

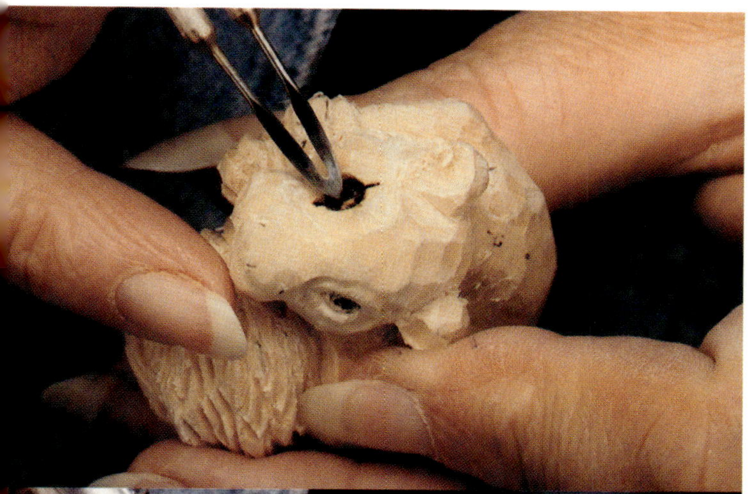

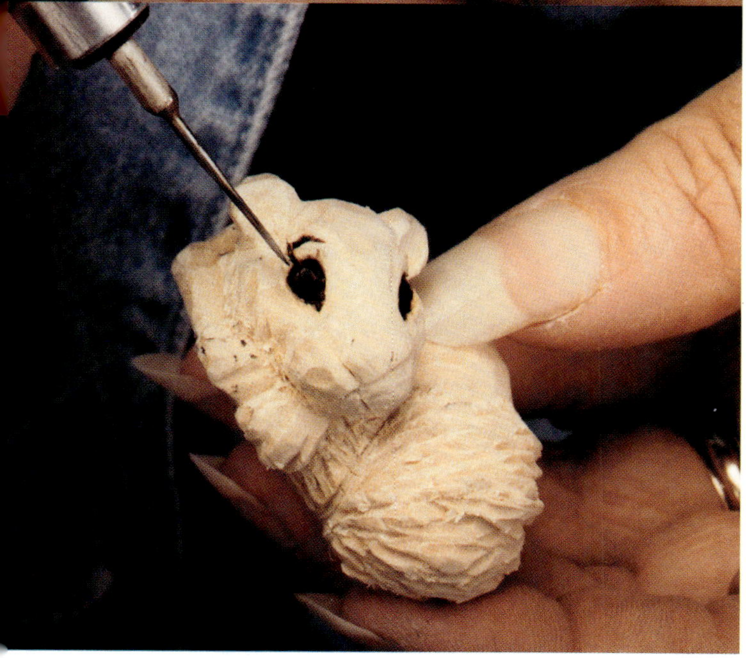

Use a pointed wood burning tip to outline the eyeball, then burn the eyeball and tear duct. This will make them shiny and distinct when painted.

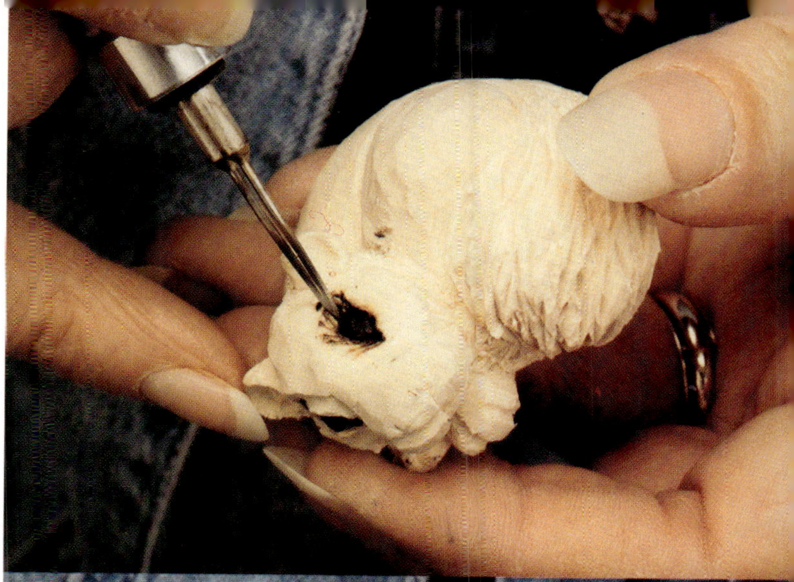

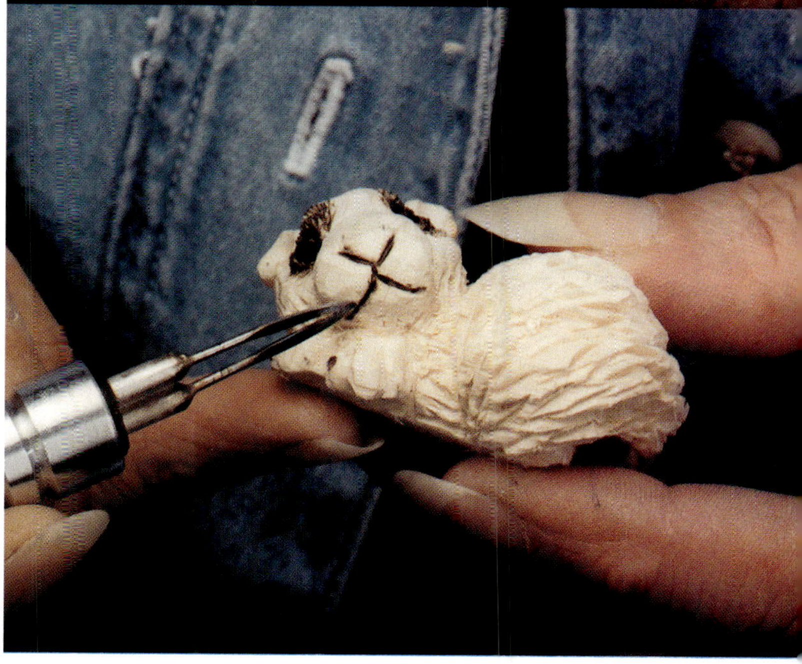

Using short strokes, begin to add hair around the eyes. Study animals to see the natural hair growth patterns of each animal. Outline the nose with the wood burner...and around the mouth.

Take little, short strokes around the head where the hair is shorter.

Putting in dots to represent whiskers.

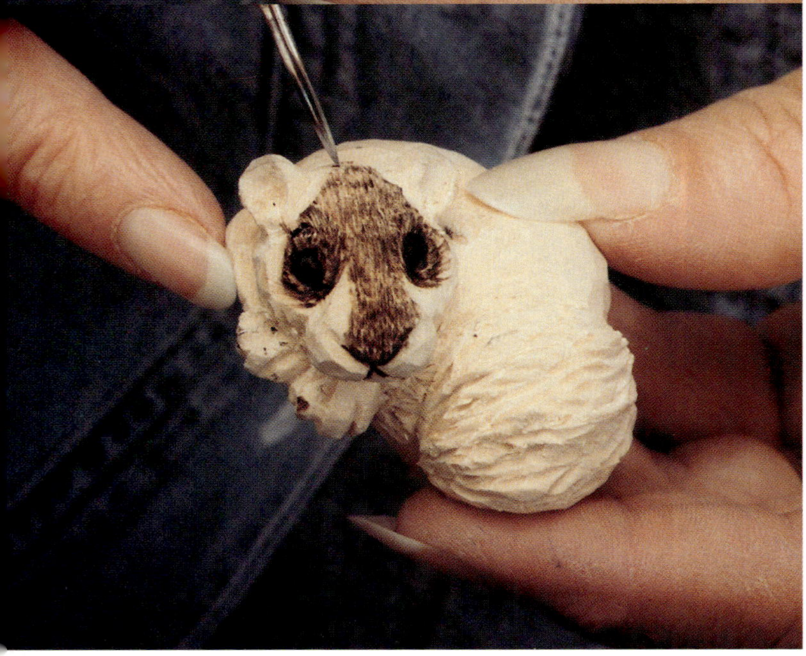

Continuing to burn in the short fur along the head.

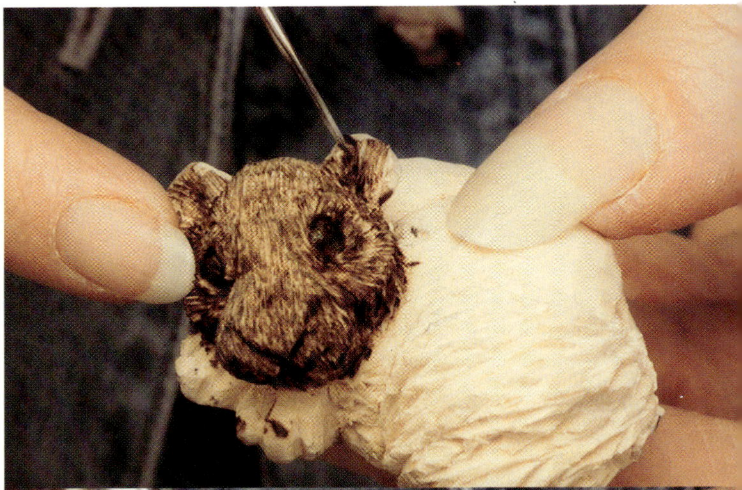

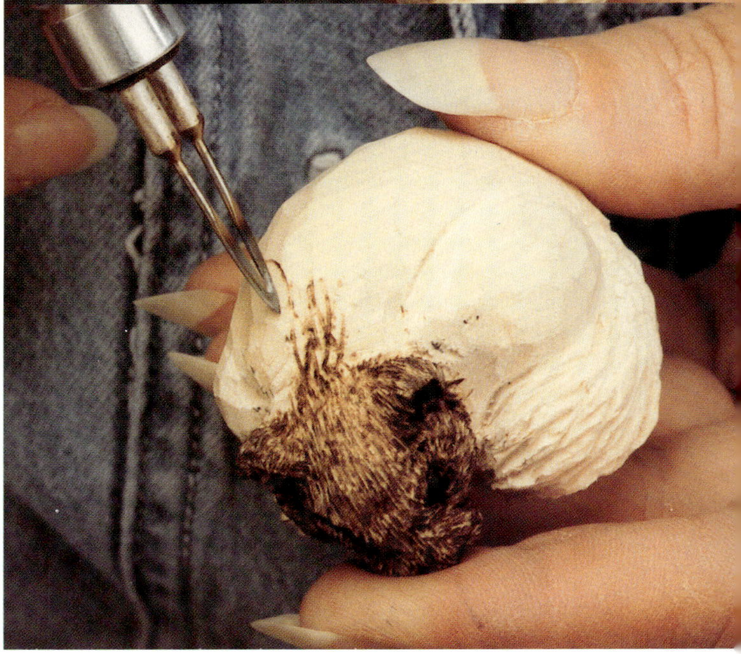

Burn in around the ear and inside the ear. Move on down the spine.

Use longer strokes on the body, making sure that the fur lines do not run parallel, giving the animal a brushed appearance.

Burn in between the toes.

To create claws, burn in a triangle at the end of each toe. The burnt claws will make the toes stronger and less prone to breaking.

Burn in the rest of the fur on the toes.

To burn in the tail, burn across the V tool lines cut into the tail. This will give the tail additional depth and "fluff."

The wood burning is complete.

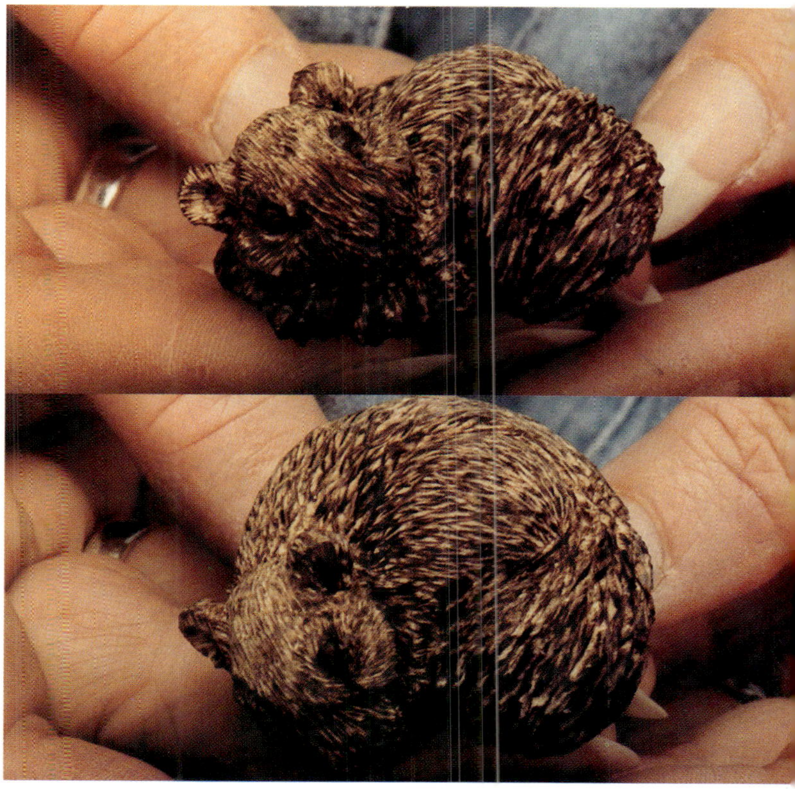

Carving the Black Bear

The bear we will carve. The walnut is so beautiful, we will not paint this carving.

Using a 2" x 1" walnut blank, we're going to carve a black bear.

The head is now fully exposed.

Round the blank and add the outline of the head and the curve of the spine as guides.

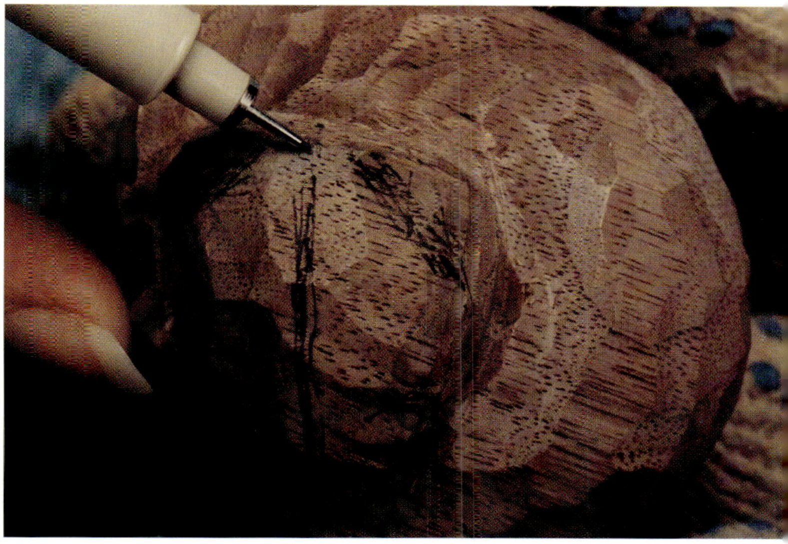

Draw in the centerline and the lines for the muzzle and the ears.

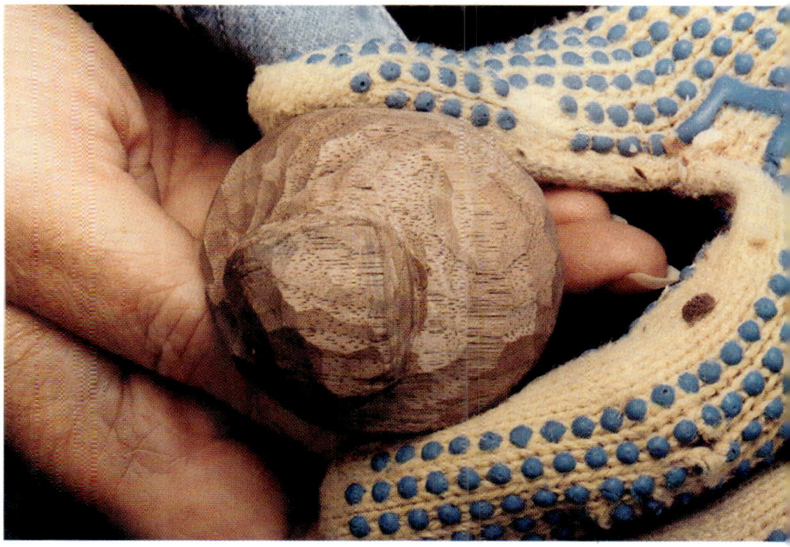

Remove the background wood away from the head.

Using the 3/16" veiner, follow the guidelines and begin to define and round the muzzle.

Round the end of the muzzle.

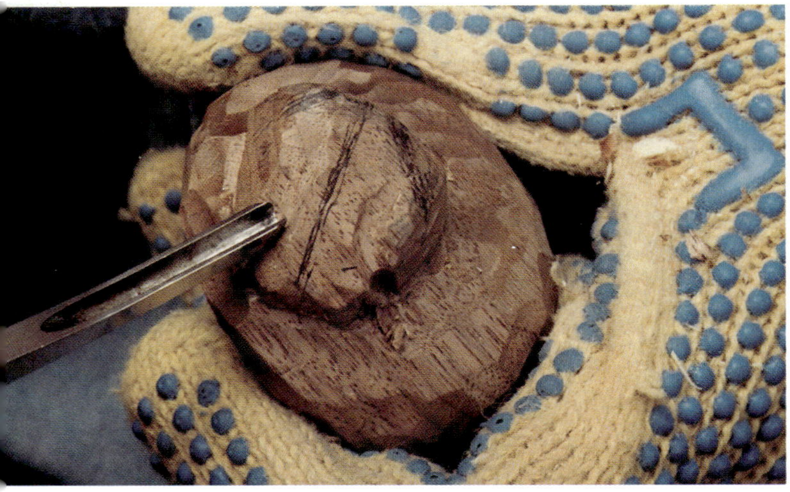

Now cut up along the sides of the muzzle to the eyes.

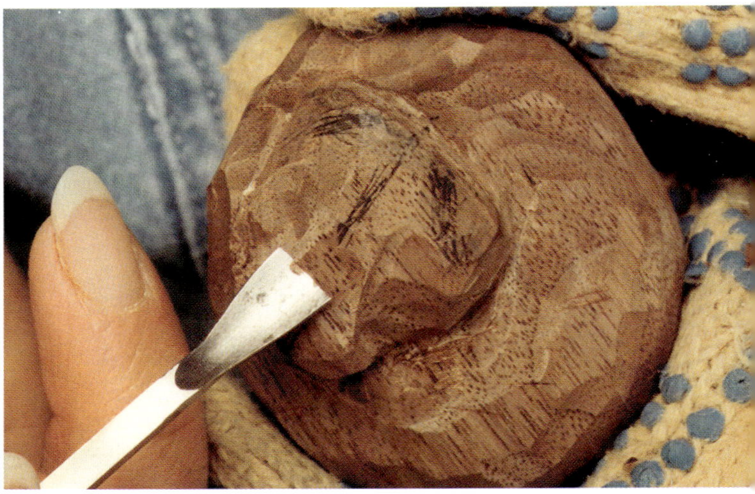

Use the #7 gouge to further reduce the size and shape of the black bear's nose. Its nose is similar to that of a large dog.

Cut down along the sides of the head with a #7 gouge to make the muzzle stand out.

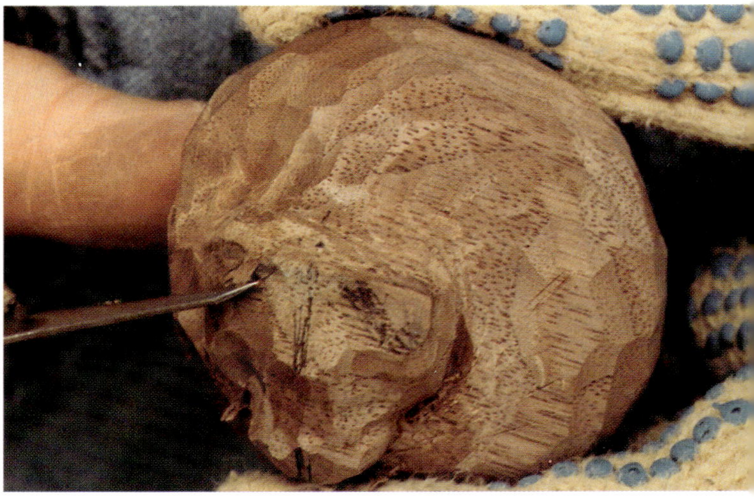

Draw diagonal lines on top of the head to indicate where the ears should be.

Cut the background wood away. Put in a stop cut along the line of the ears and cut away the excess wood in front of each ear.

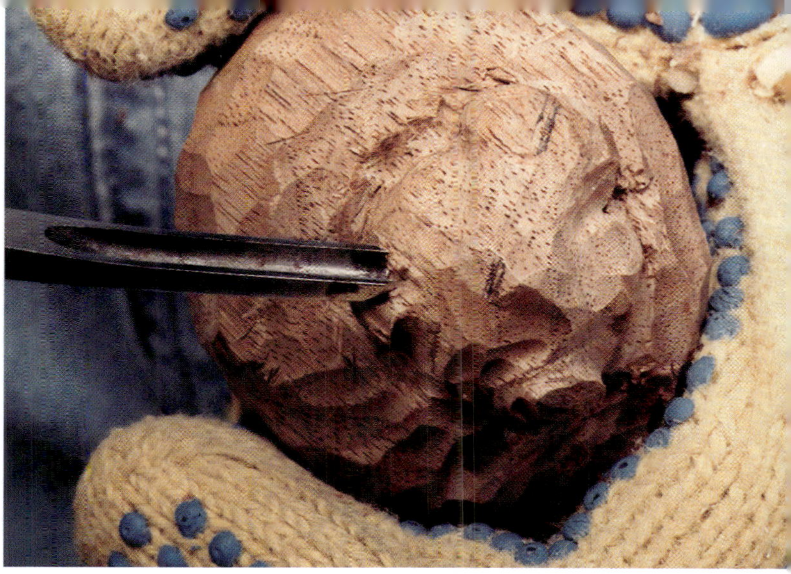

Use the veiner to hollow out the insides of the ears as well.

Remove wood from the forehead and from between the ears to push the ears up. In this image I am currently removing excess wood from between the ears. The head is facing forward.

The inside of the ear is hollowed out. Also carve out a hollow in front of the ears, creating this animal's temples. Be very careful when hollowing out the ears so as not to break them.

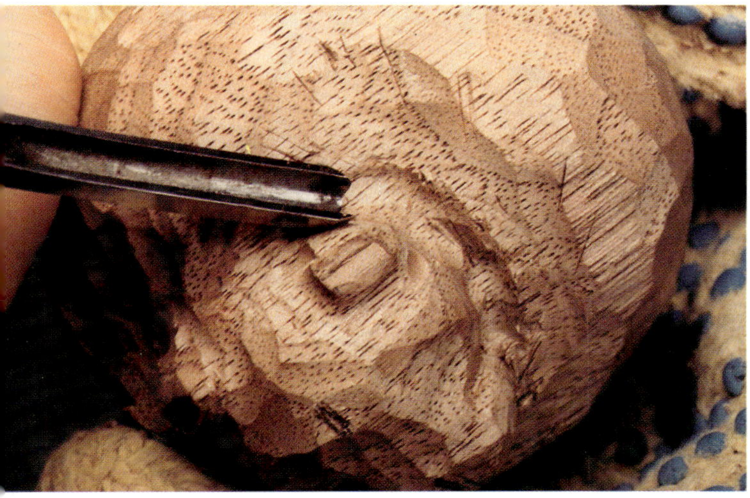

Use the veiner to carve in the neck and the backs of the ears.

Use the knife to continue shaping the ears and the head. Remove sharp edges.

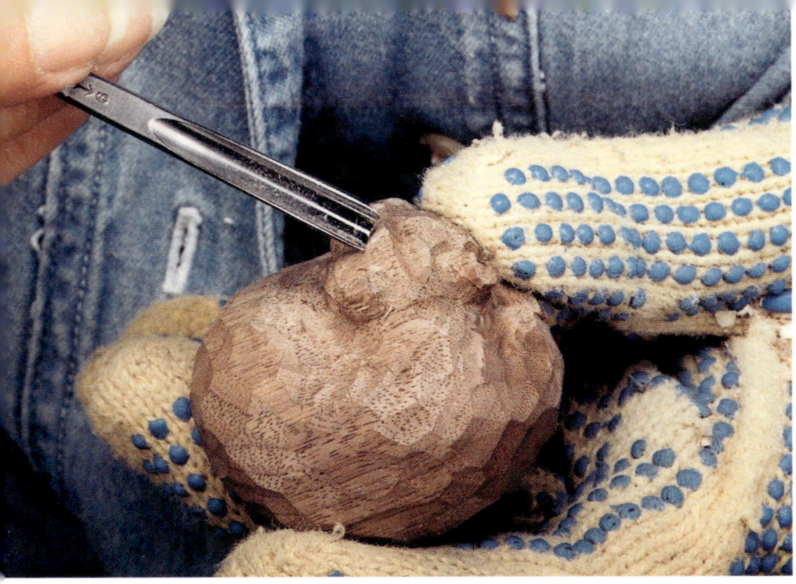

Bears often have a hair part in the middle of their foreheads. Carve this in with a 5 mm #9 gouge. Hollow out the eyes a little further with this gouge.

Draw in the guidelines for the triangular nose and the mouth.

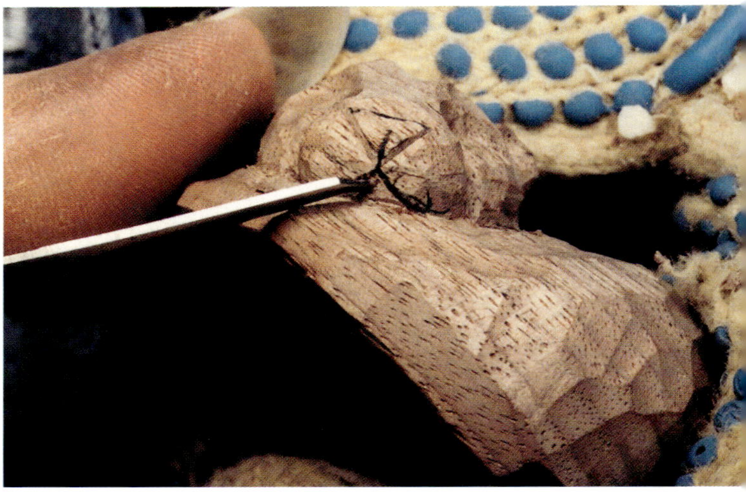

Cut around the mouth as well.

Place stop cut lines along these guides with a carving knife. Cut back around the nose pad to make it stand out.

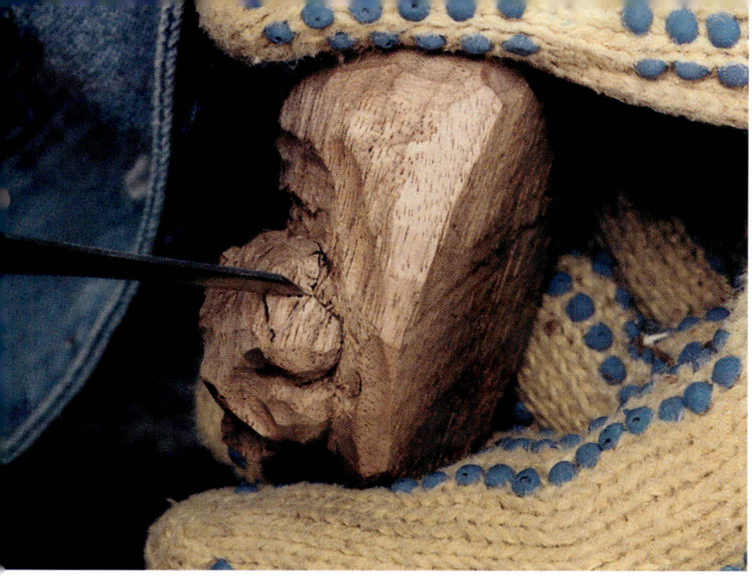

Cut in the separation in the base of the nose pad. Carve this feature in with a V cut.

Draw in sleeping bear eyes. Basically these are crescent moon shapes.

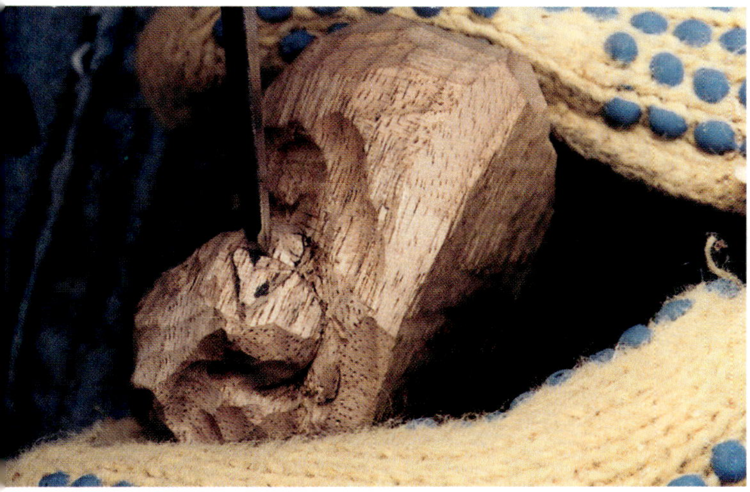

Use the smallest veiner you can get to cut in the nostrils. Cut straight in to make the shape of these tiny nostrils.

Use the smallest veiner to cut in the line of the closed eyes and small tear ducts on the insides of the eyes. The tear duct is simply a small vertical line along the inside of the eye.

The nostrils are in place.

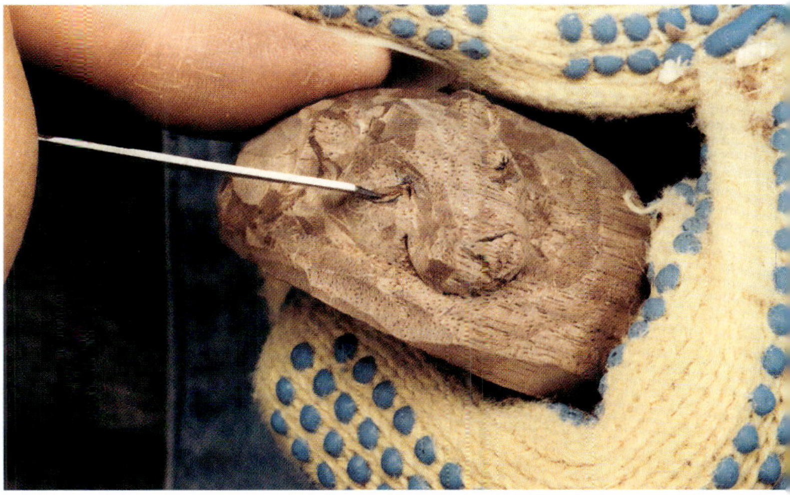

Sometimes I use a knife to open the eye line a little wider.

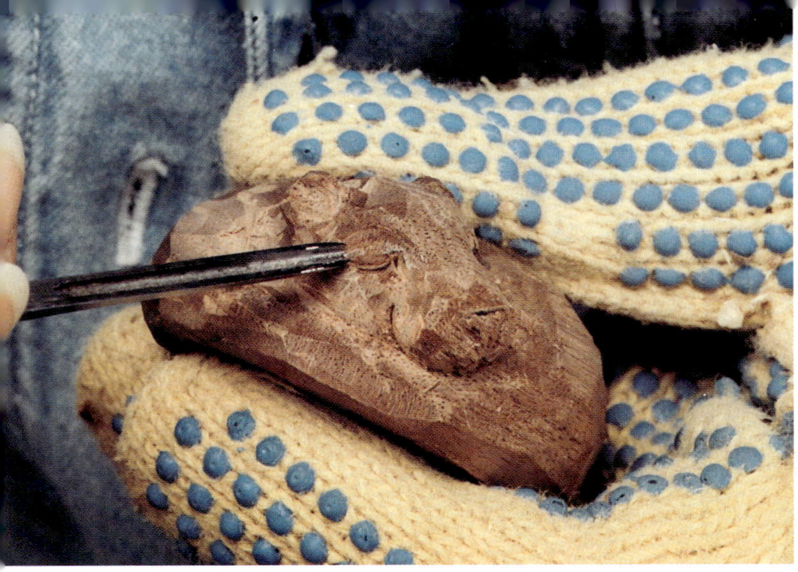

Use a #1 veiner to make a cut above the eyelid to form the eyebrow and the shape of the underlying eyeball below.

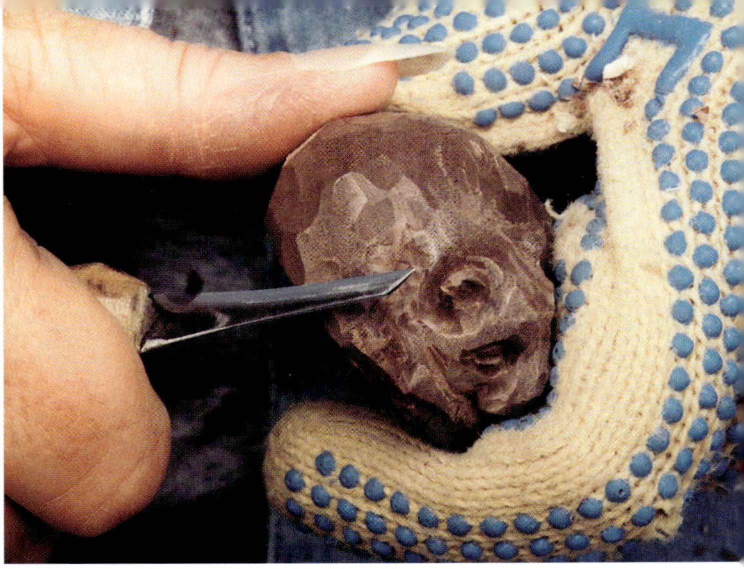

I need to take off some extra wood in front of the bear's shoulder before continuing.

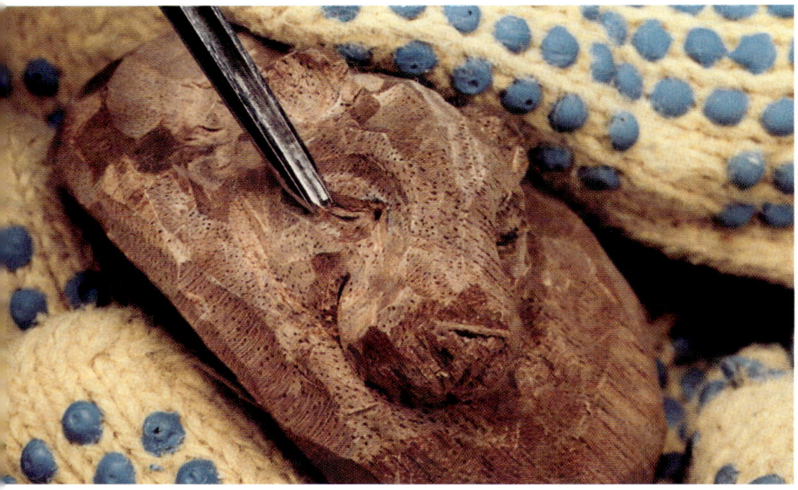

Make a similar cut under the eye to create the bag of the lower lid and to define the lower edge of the unseen eyeball.

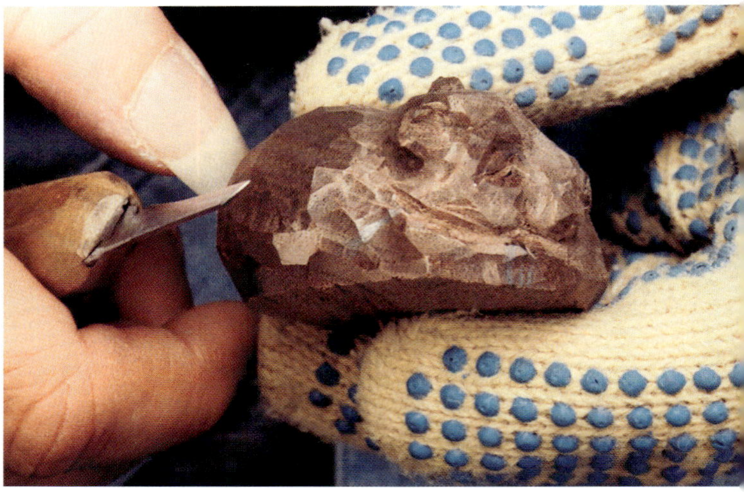

Now the shoulder is carved down to a size we can work with.

The face is now carved.

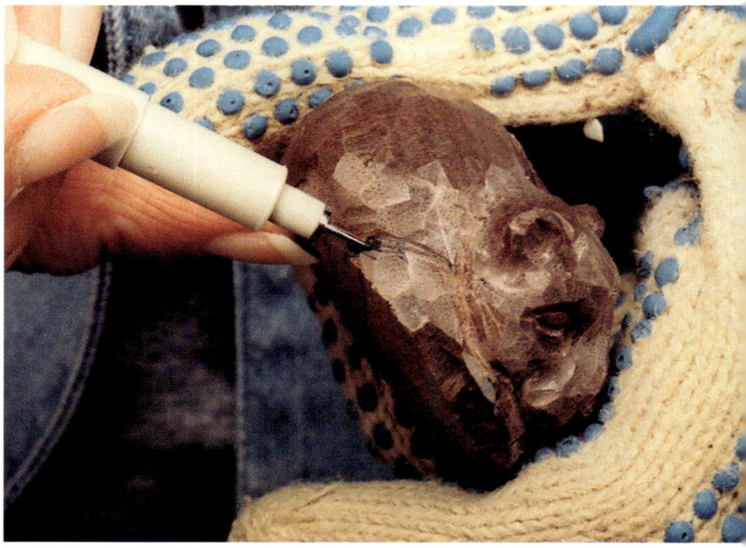

Define the area between the shoulder and the back. Draw in the guideline.

Follow the guideline with the 3/16" veiner to separate the shoulder from the body.

Using the carving knife, separate the toes from the paw. Make a V shaped cut with the knife to create the separation of the toes. A V tool can also be used.

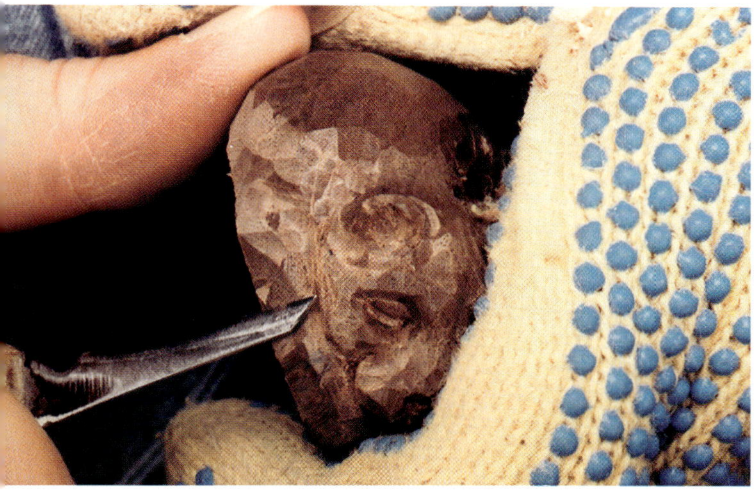

Define the angle of the elbow joint on the bear's front leg.

The toes have been separated from the paw.

Like so.

Carve away excess wood between the two paws.

Mark the area for the left shoulder, leg, and left front paw.

Remove excess wood from the body to raise the left leg above the surrounding body of the bear.

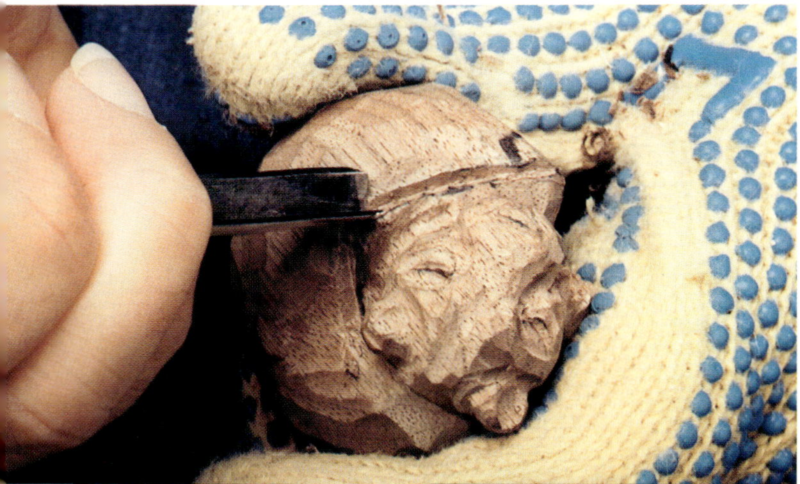

With a 1/4" V tool, cut along the guidelines for the shoulder, leg, and paw.

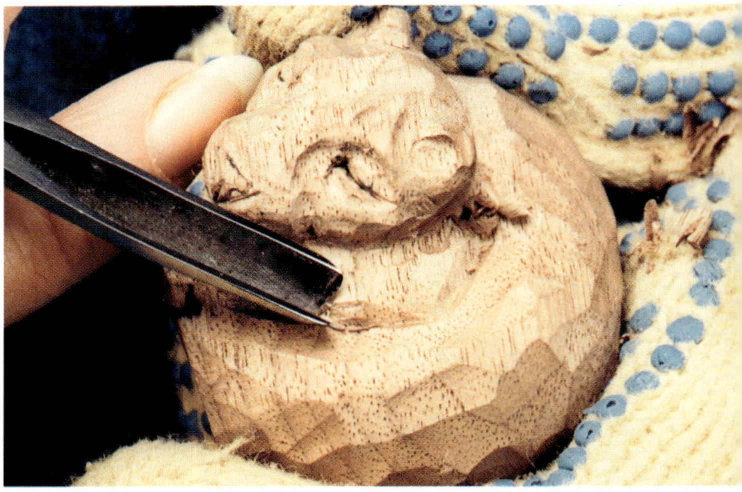

Continue to remove excess wood until you are satisfied.

The left shoulder and leg are separated from the surrounding body. The left paw is outlined.

Follow the guidelines, carve around the paw with the knife, making a series of small stop cuts to allow the paw to stand higher than the rest of the body.

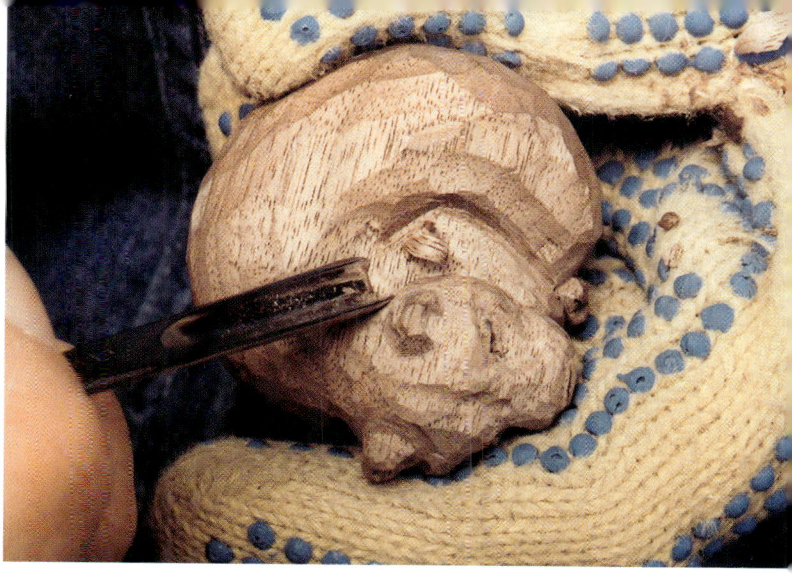

Using a gouge, go in around the jaw line and the neck to redefine them.

The paw is separated from the body.

Redraw the line of the bear's spine to make sure you get the curvature of the bear's back carved in correctly.

Cut in the separations between the toes on the left front paw with your knife.

Start to shape up the back some more, rounding it.

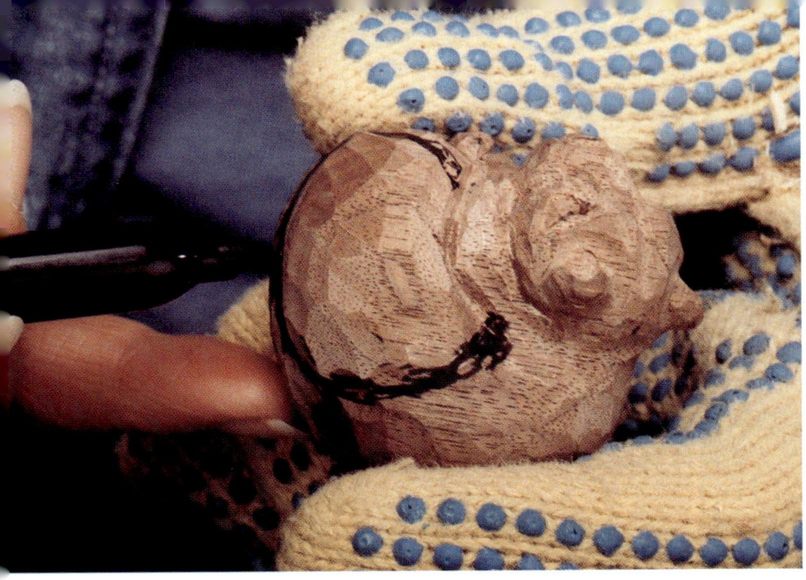

Draw in the lines defining the back hip area.

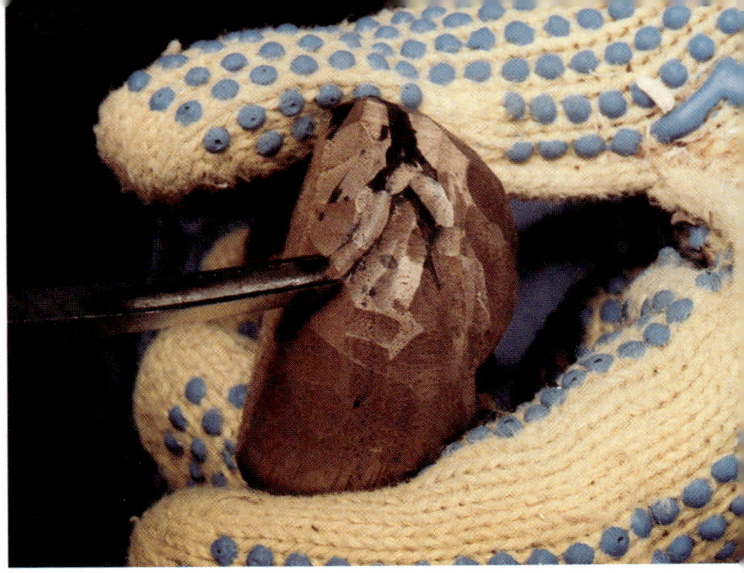

The tail of the bear is short.

Draw in the location of the tail and the back foot as well. These lines help to determine where to make the cuts.

Separating between the bear's two hind quarters.

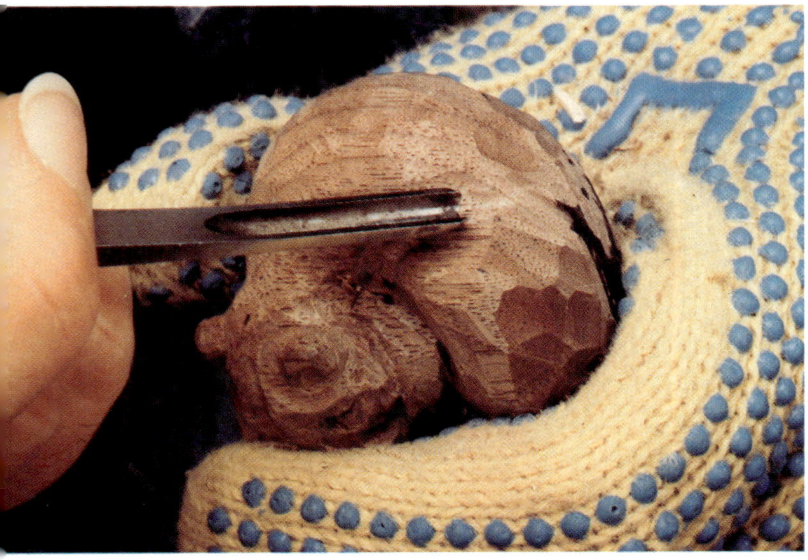

Following the line of the hip with the veiner.

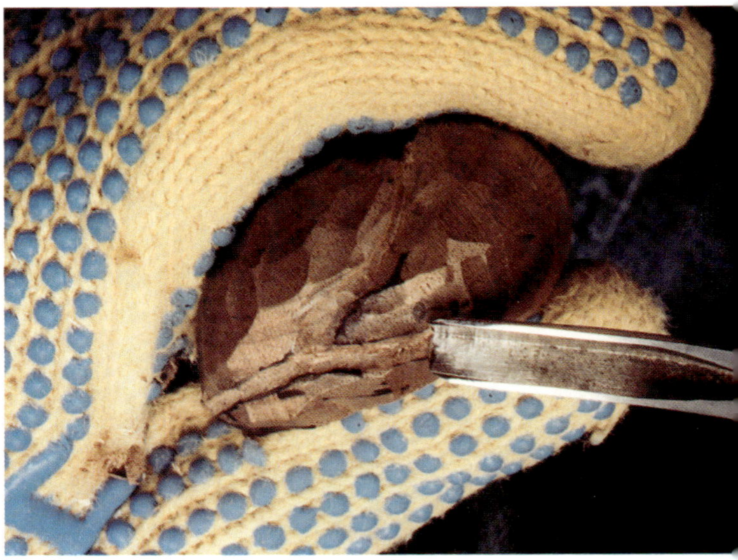

Deepen the cuts around the tail and the bear's hind quarters with a V tool.

Continue shaping the hip and body of the bear.

Reducing the size of the back paw.

Use the knife to carve in the back paw. Part of the back paw extends underneath the body.

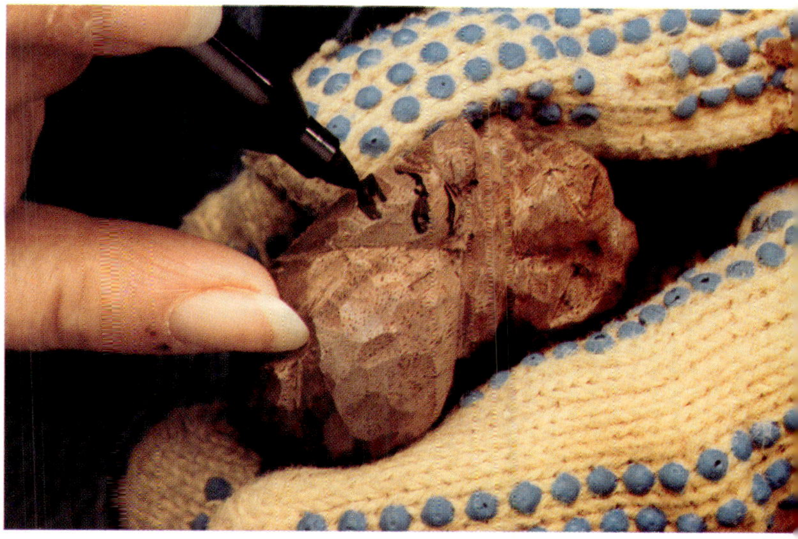

Draw in the separation of the toes on the back paw.

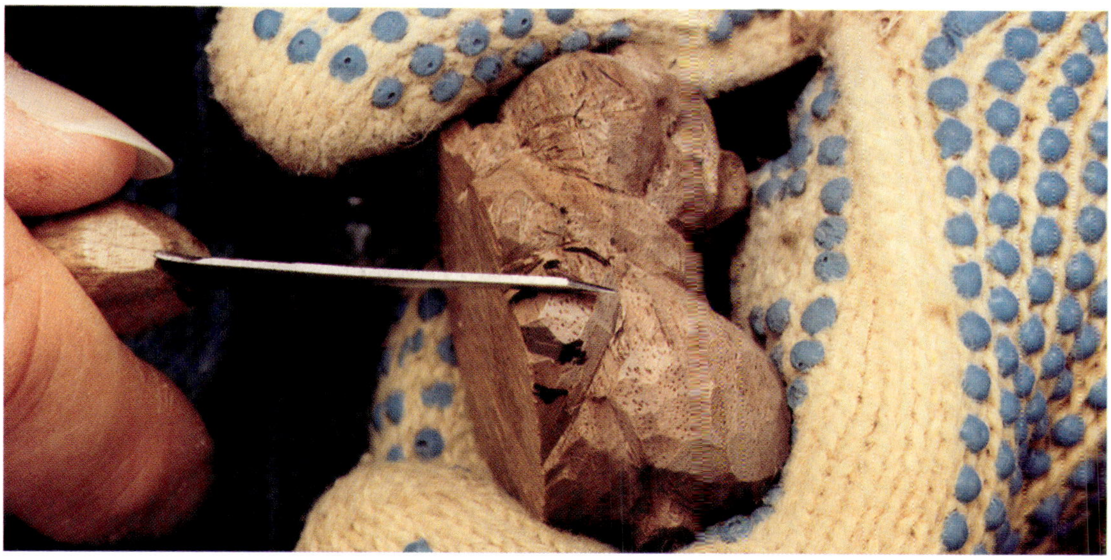

Cut in the toes with your carving knife.

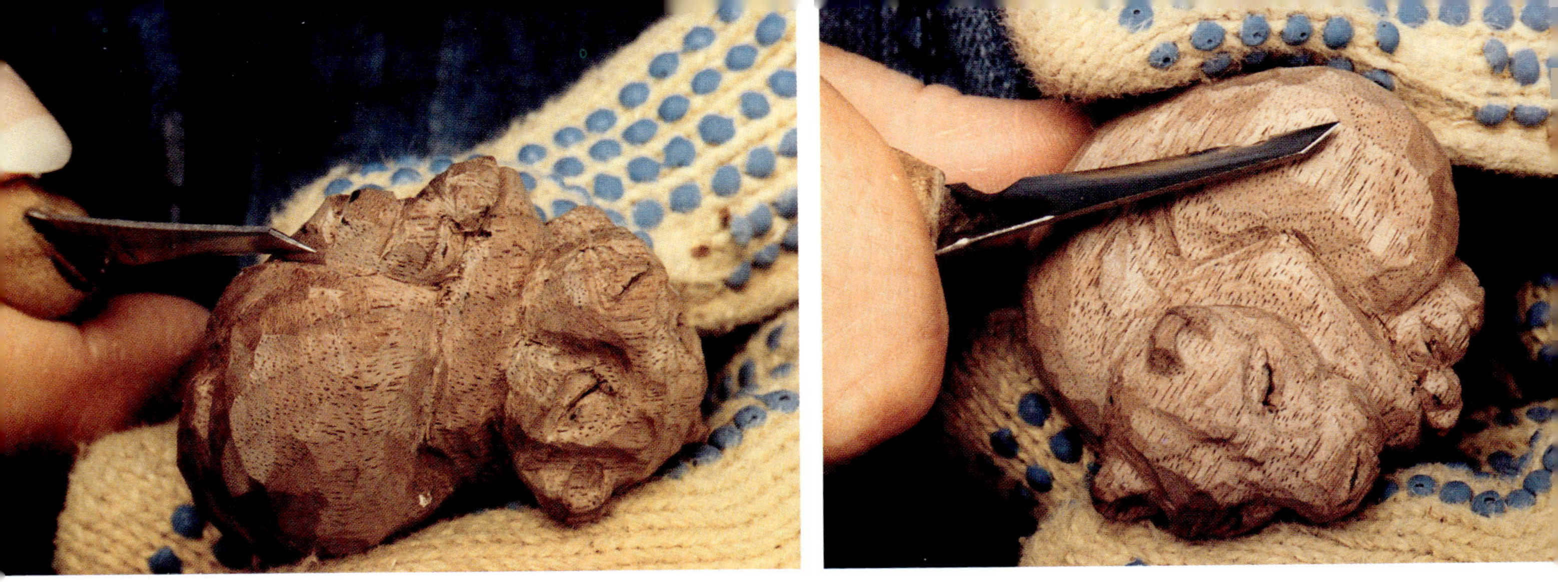

The toes on the back paw are in place. Now that all of the features are in place, continue to shape the bear until he is in proportion all around.

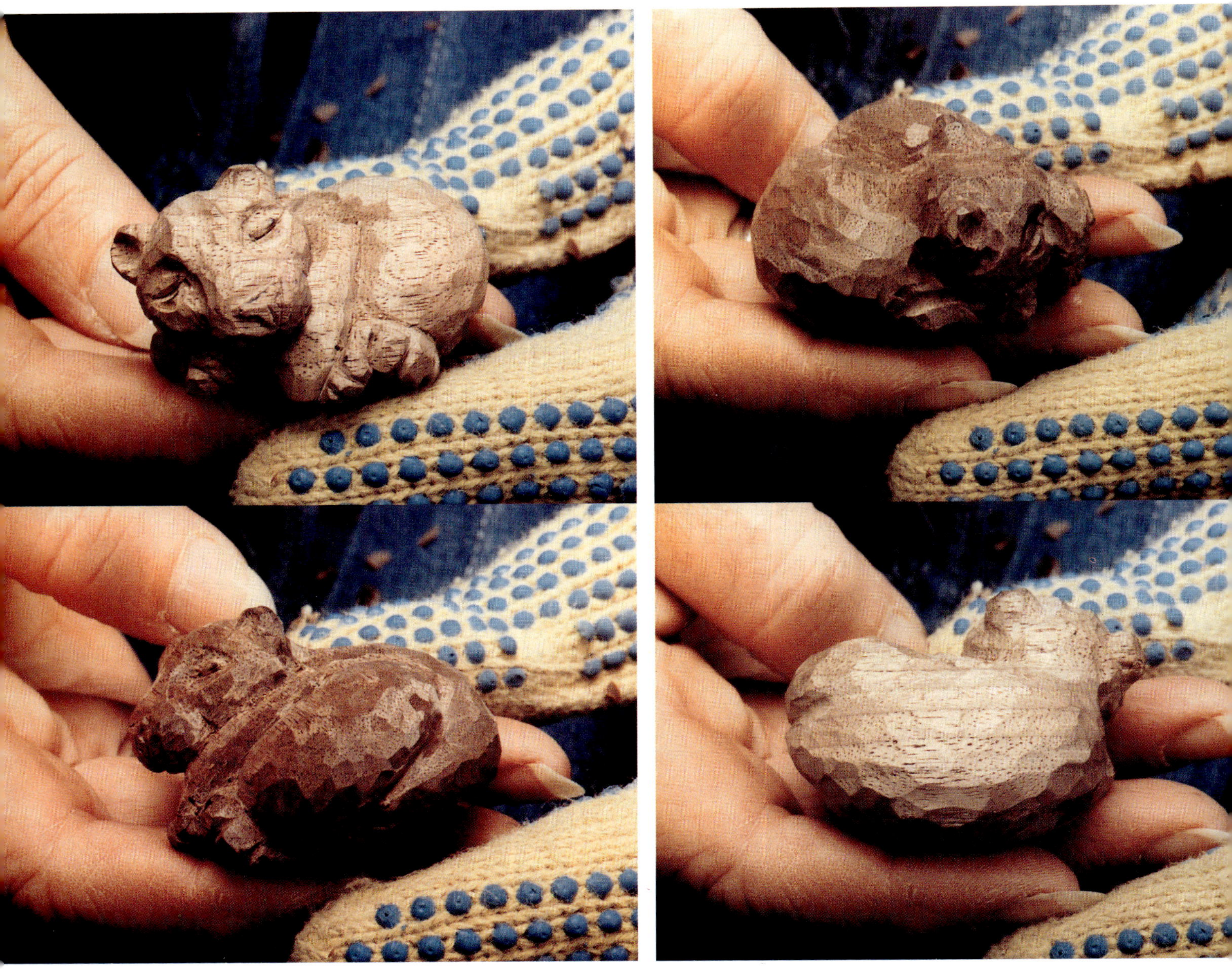

The bear is now complete. There is no need to paint this hardwood bear as the wood is beautiful all by itself. A finish of Danish Oil or Boiled Linseed Oil will bring out the beauty of the wood and protect it as well.

Painting the Squirrel & a Sleeping Mouse

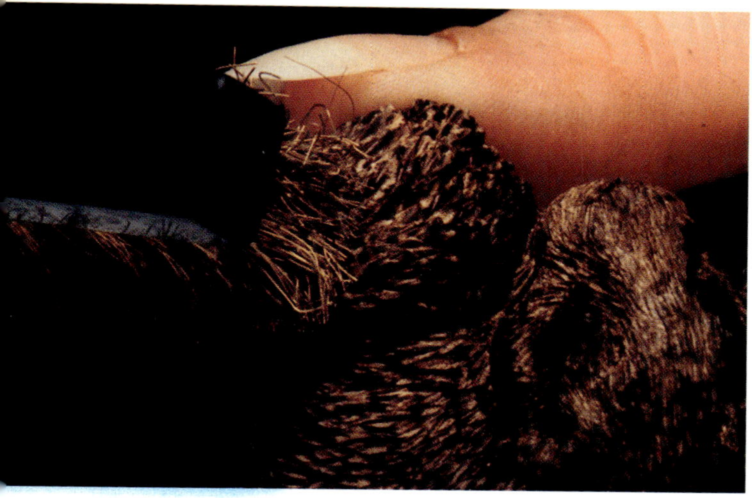

Use a brass bristled brush to remove burned wood from the squirrel carving prior to painting. It must be a brass brush because any other type of metal brush will scratch the wood.

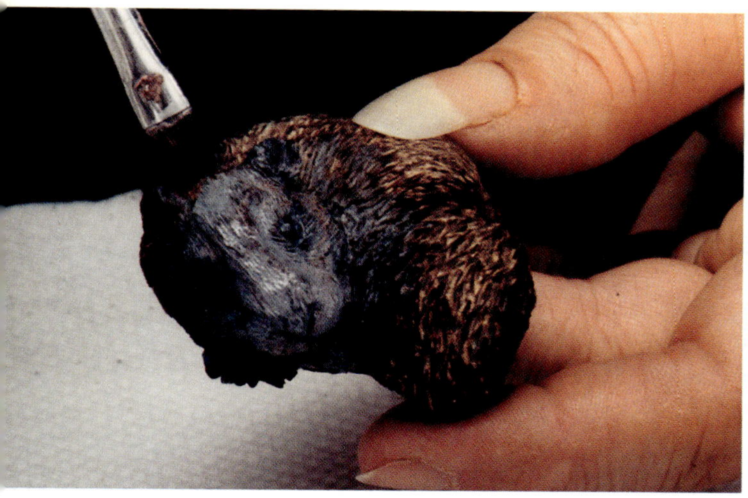

Use oil paints mixed with turpentine in a jar to create your paint washes. Keep the paint thin enough that the wood shows through it. The oil colors are easily blended together as applied. Animal fur is not uniform in color. Fur is a mix of many colors. In the squirrel you will find gray mixed with black and brown. Paint the squirrel with a gray paint wash first.

The gray paint now covers all of the squirrel including the uncarved bottom to give pieces a finished look.

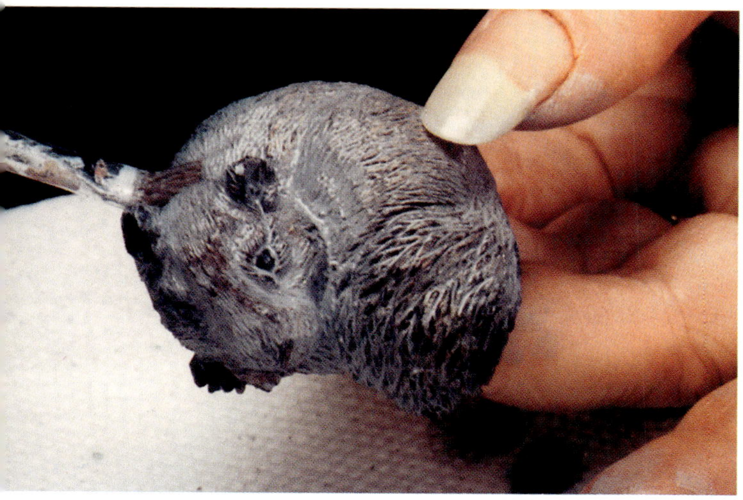

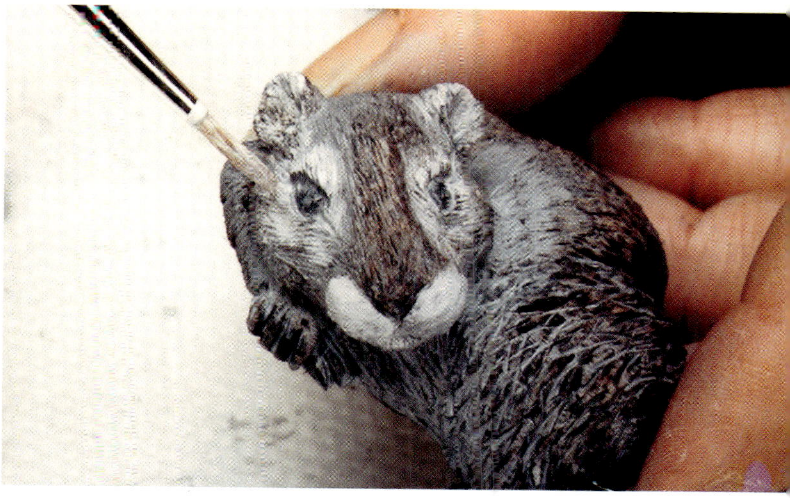

Apply some white around the muzzle, eyes ..

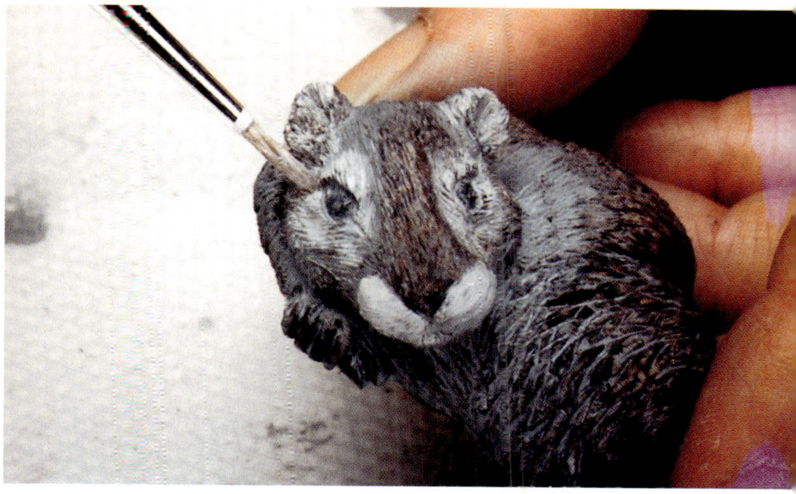

and on the outer edges of the ears.

Apply white to the tail and belly as well.

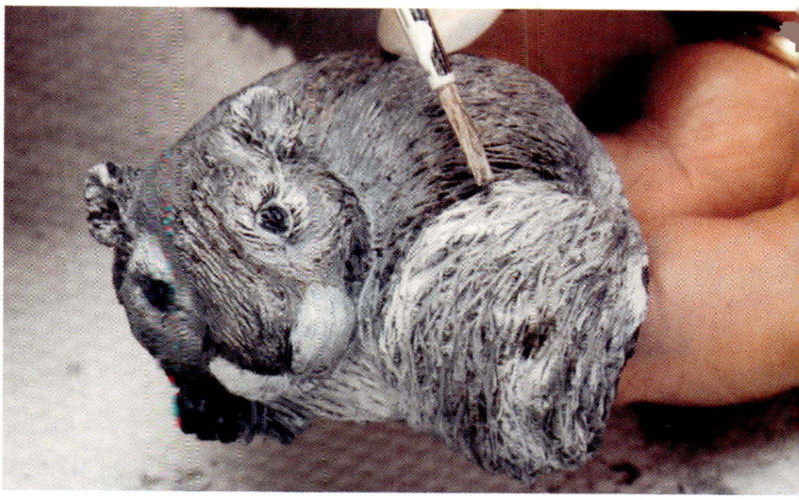

Add Burnt Sienna to the cheeks...

and on the paws.

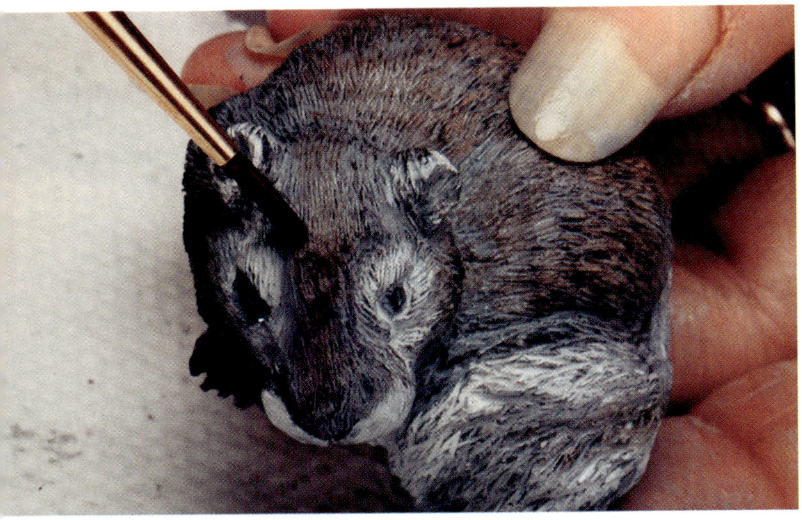

along the bridge of the nose ...

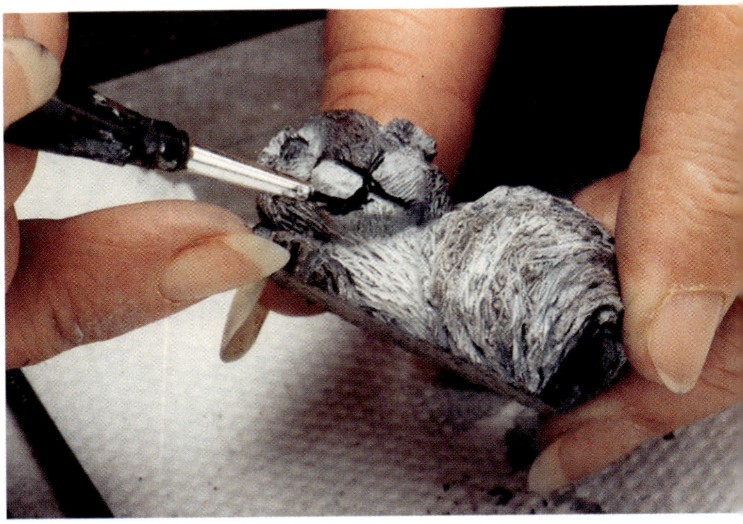

Use black to outline the separations of the nose and mouth.

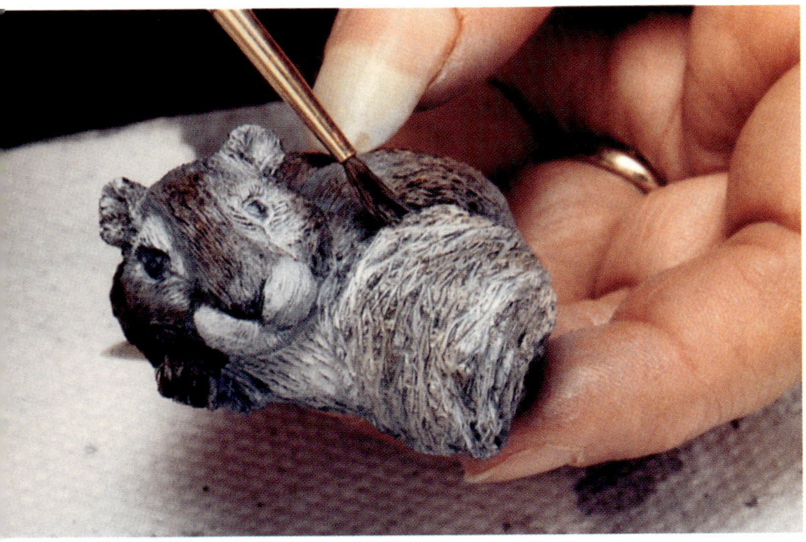

along the tail ...

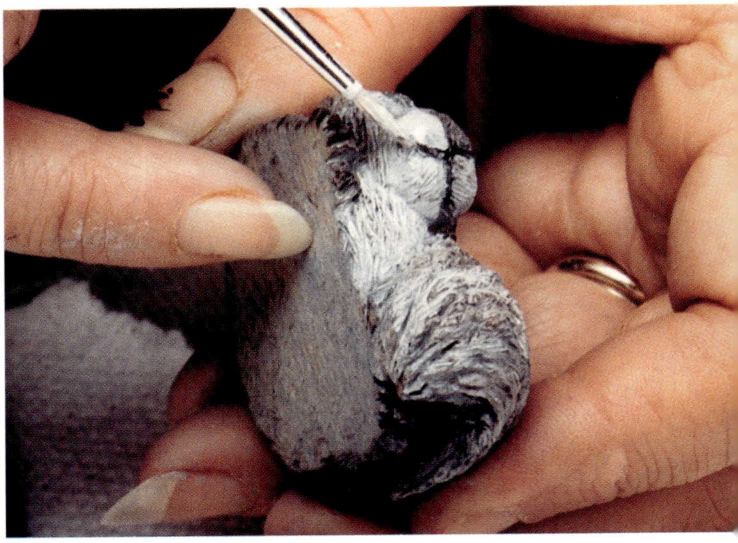

If you paint outside the lines, wait a while and go back over the area with white.

Add black dots to the muzzle to indicate whiskers.

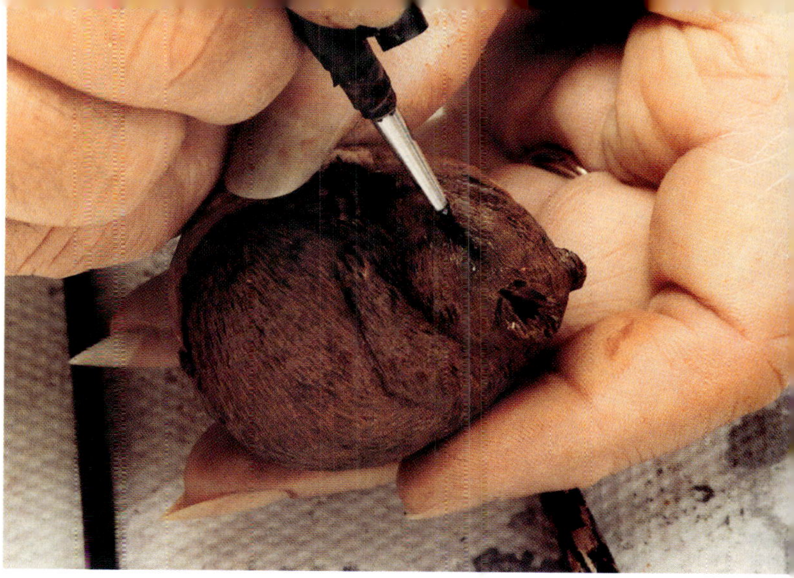

Using a little touch of black paint, outline the closed eyes to make them show up a bit better.

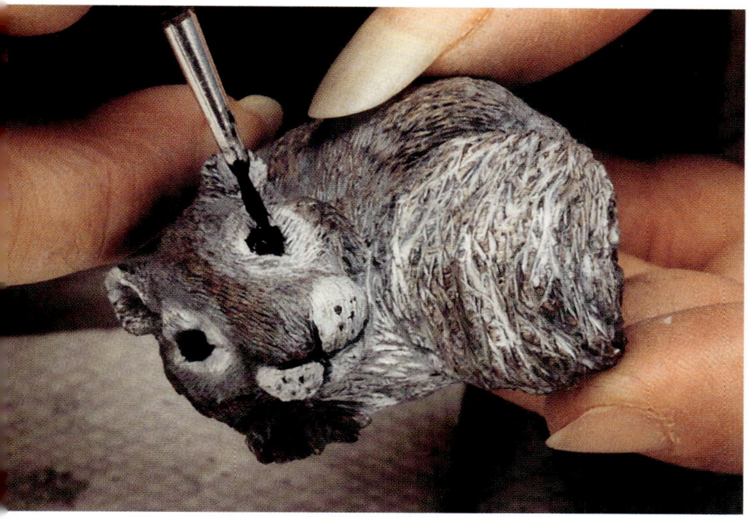

Carefully paint the eye black. Let the squirrel dry a bit and we will come back to it later.

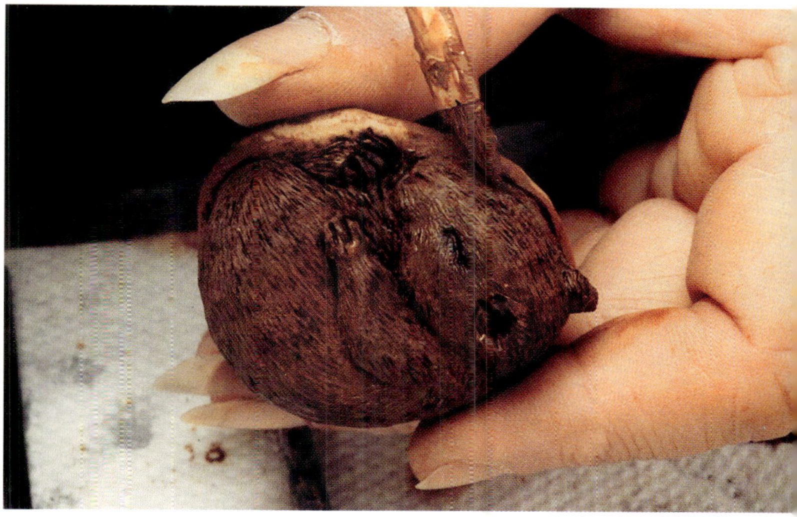

Touch up with Raw Sienna if the black bleeds.

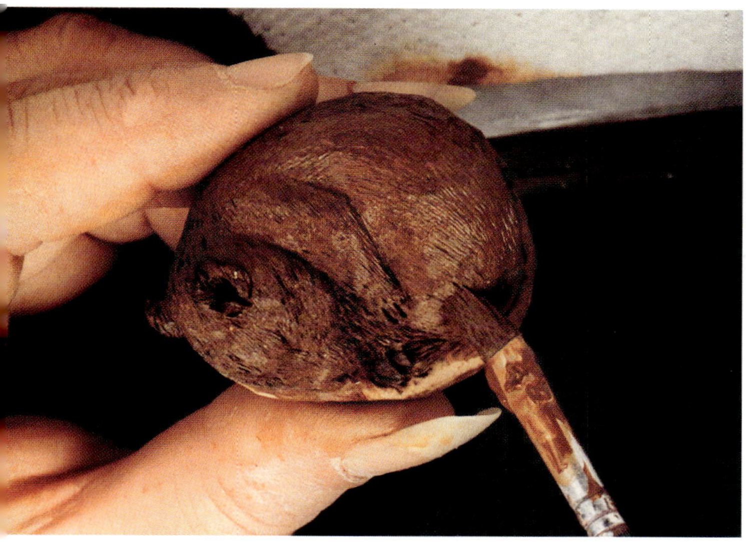

To paint a sleeping mouse, use Raw Sienna to paint the entire body first, except for the tail.

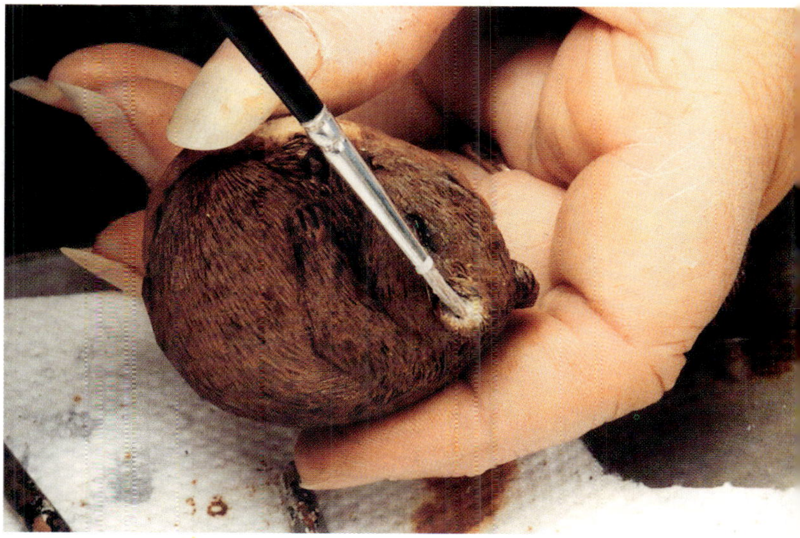

Apply a little white to the insides of the ears.

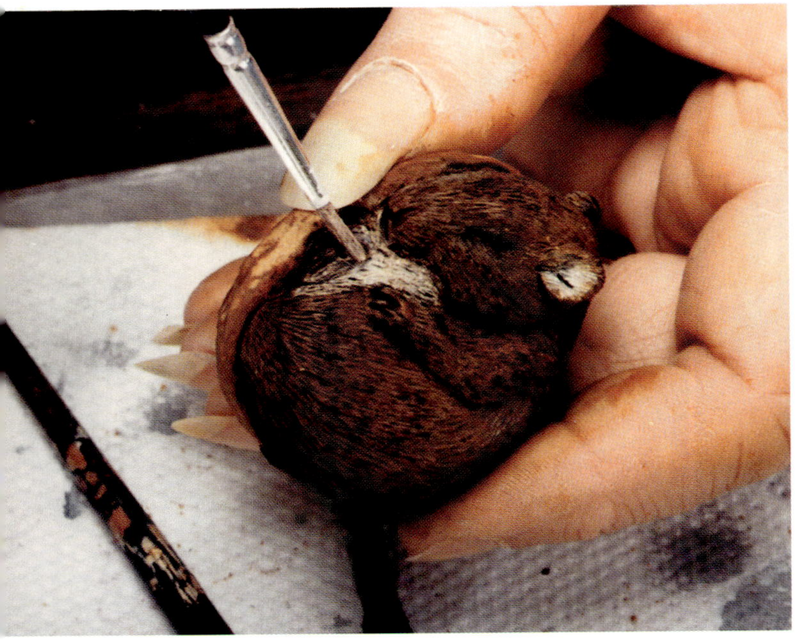

Add white to the mouse's belly as well.

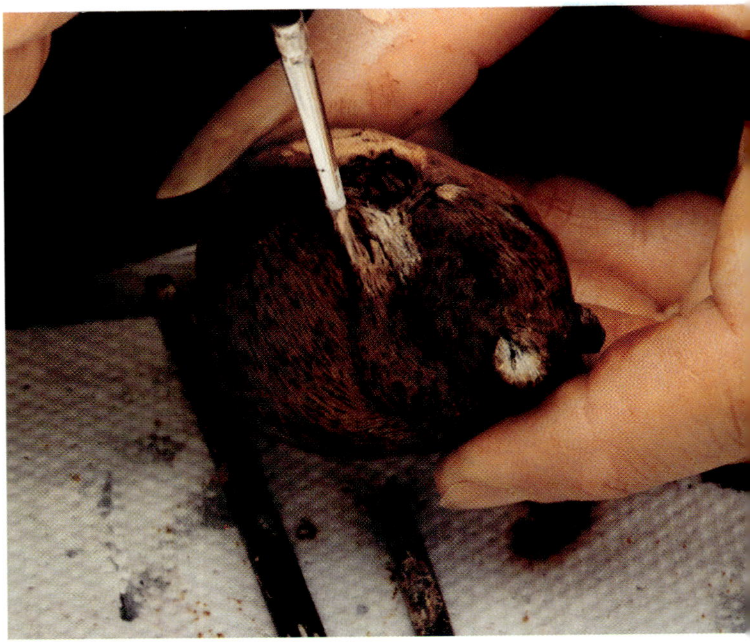

the paws ...

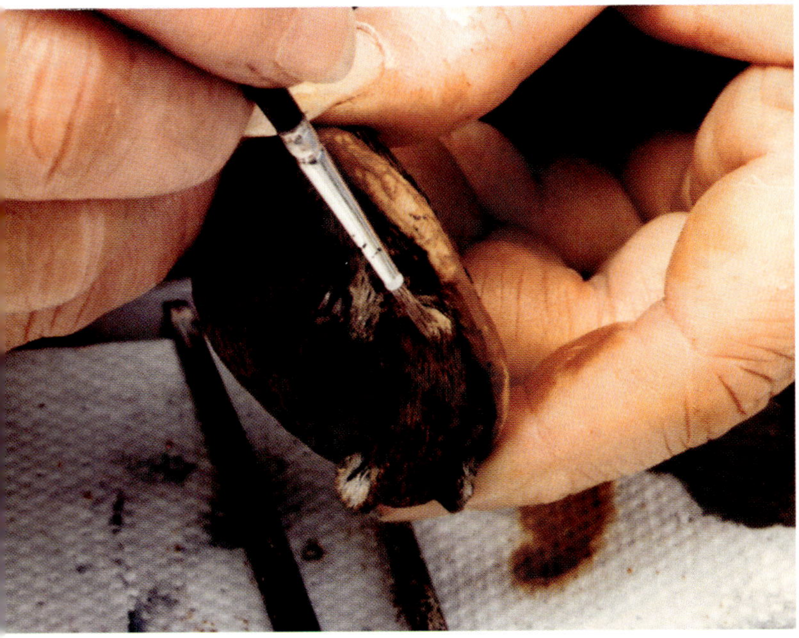

Use a pinkish flesh color on the nose ...

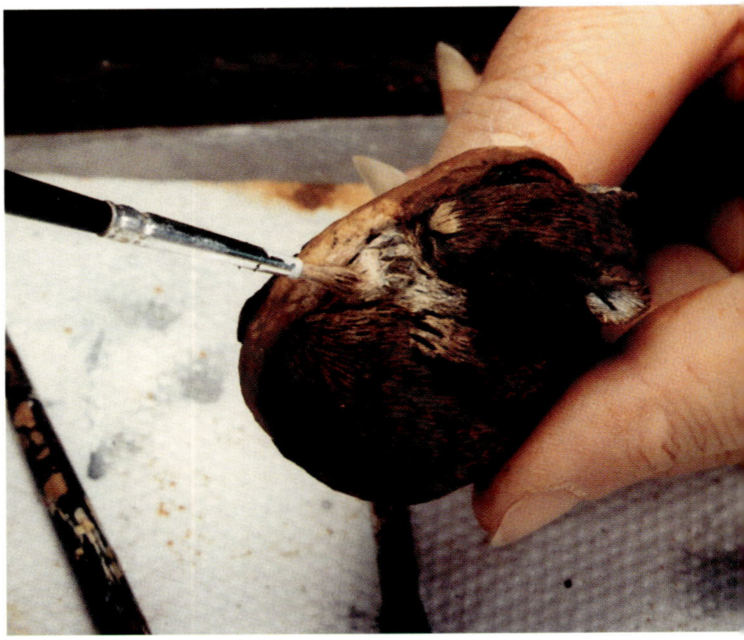

the base of the upturned hind paw ...

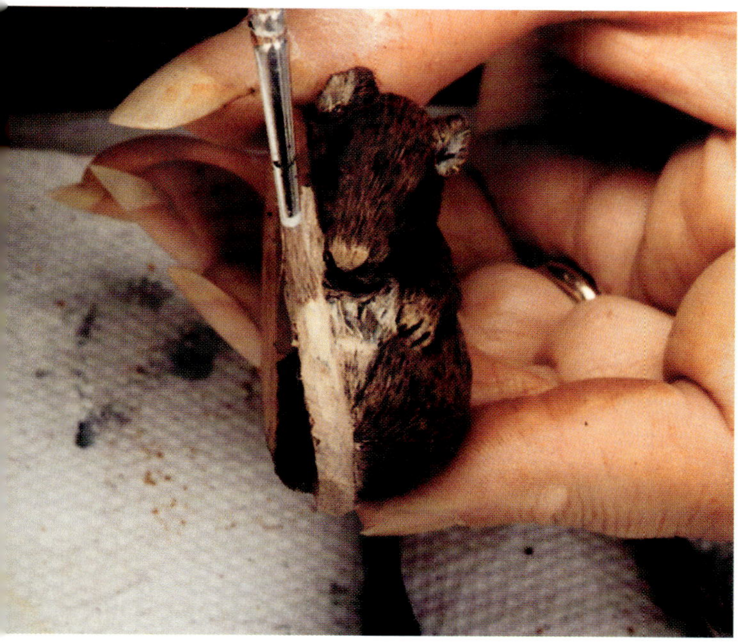

and the tail.

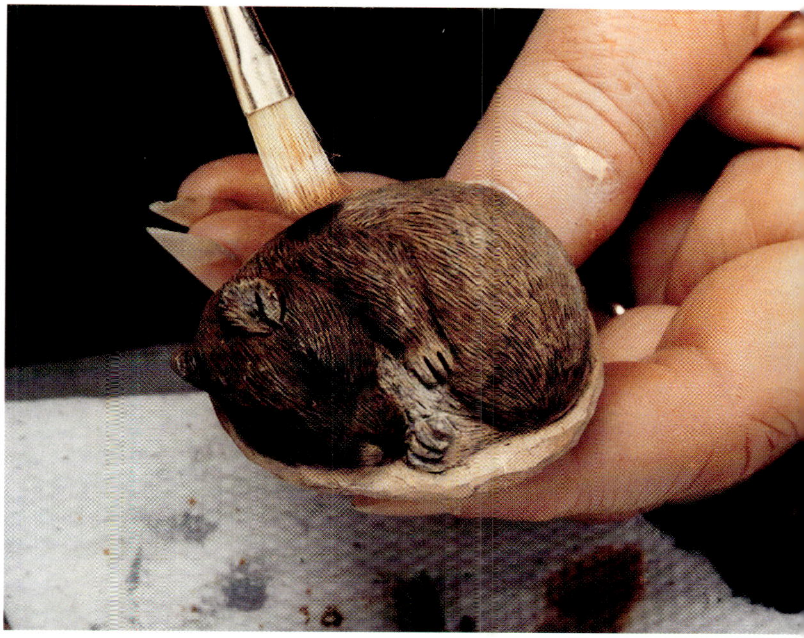

To dry brush, use white straight from the tube onto the bristles. Rub the brush bristles on a paper towel to remove most of the paint. Brush the now nearly dry bristles across the back and head, applying small amounts of white paint to any part of the body that would normally catch the sunlight and create highlights. This technique also pulls all the colors together.

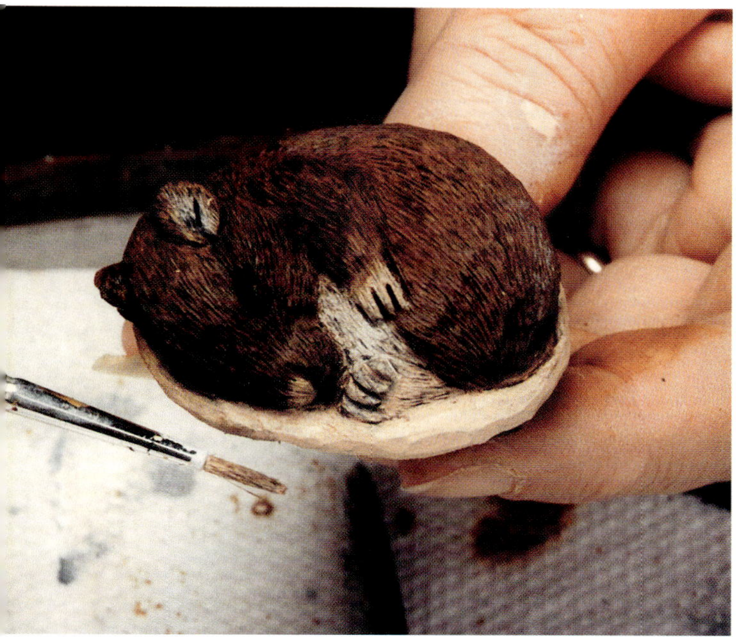

Except for the dry brushing, this mouse is complete.

The dry brushing on the mouse is complete.

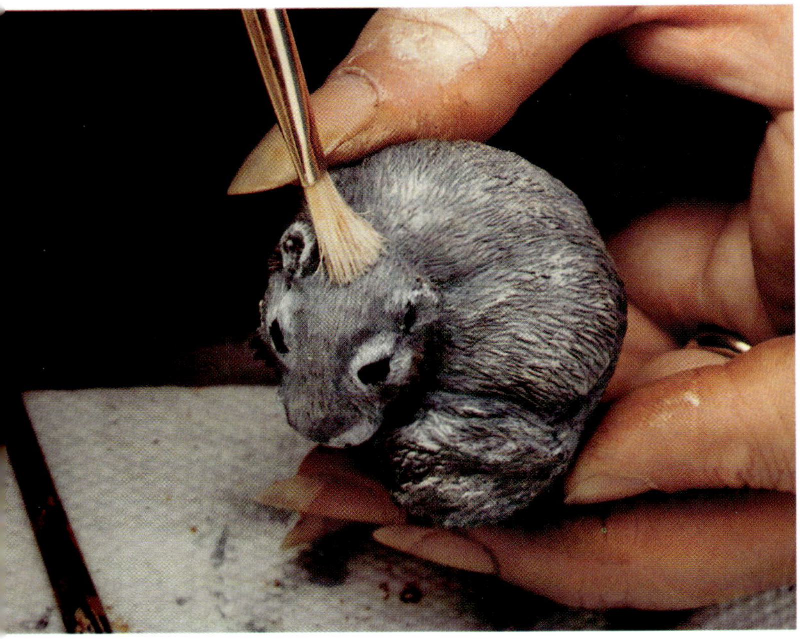

Dry brushing the squirrel.

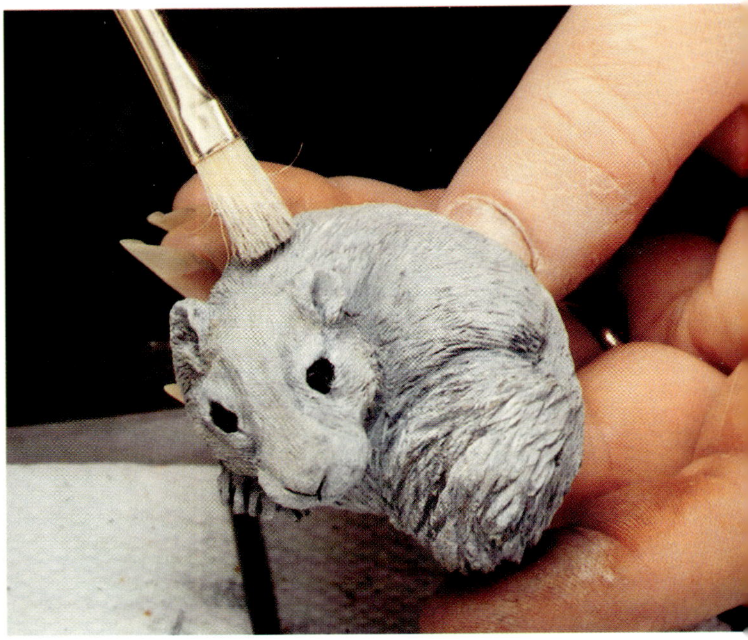

The dry brushing is done.

Using a toothpick and undiluted white paint, add highlights to the squirrel's eyes in give them life. Spray the finished carving with a coat of Deft or any other acryllic matte or semi-gloss spray to protect it.

Gallery